TESTING THE KITE-STRING SAILBOAT

MANUAL TRAINING TOYS
for the BOY'S WORKSHOP

by Harris W. Moore

Linden Publishing Inc.
Fresno, CA

DEDICATED
TO THE BOY WHO LIKES
TO TINKER ROUND

MANUAL TRAINING TOYS
for the BOY'S WORKSHOP

© 2009 Linden Publishing Inc.

135798642

ISBN 13: 978-1-933502-25-0

Printed in the USA
Originally published in 1912

Other titles in this series:
The Art of Whittling
Speed Toys for Boys
Wonders in Wood
40 Power Tools You Can Make

CIP information is available from the publisher.

Linden Publishing Inc.
2006 S. Mary
Fresno CA
www.lindenpub.com
800-345-4447

CONTENTS.

CONTENTS.—(*Continued.*)

INTRODUCTION.

The wise man learns from the experience of others. That is the reason for this introduction—to tell the boy who wants to make the toys described in this book some of the "tricks of the trade." It is supposed, however, that he has had some instruction in the use of tools.

This book is written after long experience in teaching boys, and because of that experience, the author desires to urge upon his younger readers two bits of advice: First, study the drawing carefully,—every line has a meaning; second, printed directions become clearer by actually taking the tool in hand and beginning to do the work described.

BENCH.

If he buys the vise-screw, an ambitious boy can make a bench that will answer his needs, provided, also, that he can fasten it to floor or wall. It should be rigid. A beginner will find a hard wood board, 10"x2"x¼", fastened to the forward end of the bench, a more convenient stop than the ordinary bench-dog. If he has a nicely finished bench, he should learn to work without injuring the bench. A *cutting board* should always be at hand to chisel and pound upon and to save the bench-top from all ill use. The *bench-hook* should have one side for sawing and one for planing, the former having a block shorter than the width of the board so that the teeth of the saw, when they come thru the work, will strike the bench-hook rather than the bench-top.

MARKING TOOLS.

To measure accurately, hold the *ruler* on its edge so that the divisions on the scale come close to the thing measured. Let the pencil or knife point make a dash on the thing measured which would exactly continue the division line on the ruler. If it can be avoided, never use the end of the ruler; learn to measure from some figure on the ruler.

The spur of the *gage* should be filed like a knife point. It seldom stands at zero of the scale, hence, when setting the gage for accurate work, measure from the block to the spur with a ruler. The gage is a rather difficult tool for a boy to use but it will pay to master it. It may be used wherever square edges are to be made, but chamfers and bevels should be marked with a pencil.

In laying out work, the beam (the thick part) of the *trysquare* should always be kept on either the working-face or the working-edge. (See page 13, Directions for Planing.) Let the blade rest flat on any surface. Hold the trysquare snugly to the work with the fingers and thumb acting much like a bird's claw.

For accurate work (e. g. joints), lines should be drawn (scored) with the sharp point of a small *knife* blade, held nearly straight up from the edge of the trysquare blade.

Circles are located by two lines crossing at the center.

SAWS.

The teeth of a *rip-saw* are like so many little chisels set in a row; they pare the wood away. The teeth of a *crosscut-saw* are like knife points, they score two lines, and the wood breaks off between them. Large sawing should be done on a saw-horse so that the worker is over his work. If it is necessary to hold work in the vise to rip it, hold it slanting, so that the handle of the saw leads the line, as it naturally does when the work is on a saw-horse.

The *back-saw,* tho a crosscut-saw, may be used in any direction of the grain.

Any saw should be in motion when it touches the wood it is to cut. To guide it to the right place, a workman lets his thumb touch the saw just above the teeth, the hand resting firmly on the wood. A little notch, cut in the edge right to the line where the saw is to cut, will help a beginner to start accurately. Saws are rapid tools, and it pays to go slowly enough with them to do accurate work. Plan the work so as to make as few cuts as possible.

Turning-saws are best used so that the cutting is done on the pull stroke, keeping the two hands near together. When one handle is turned, the other must be turned equally.

PLANES.

Generally being in a hurry to get work done, boys are apt to take big shavings with a plane. This results in rough work. Fine shavings are better. If the plane is allowed to rest level on the work, it will find the high places without continual adjusting. The first two inches of a stroke are the hardest to plane; to plane these, press harder on the forward end of the plane. Start the plane level. Usually it is best to keep the plane straight, or nearly so, in the direction of the push.

The *block-plane* is properly used to plane the end of wood. (See page 12 on Holding Work.) On other small surfaces, however, it is often more convenient than a large plane.

BITS.

Auger-bits are numbered by the number of sixteenths in the diameter of the hole they bore, e. g. No. 4 bores a 4/16″ hole. *Gimlet-bits* are numbered by thirty-seconds.

Whenever boring with an auger-bit, stop as soon as the spur pricks thru the other side, turn the work over, start the spur in the little hole it made, and finish boring. It will always split the wood, if the bit is allowed to go way thru. It is difficult to bore a hole straight thru a piece of wood, because to tell whether the bit is held straight when starting the hole, one must look at it from two directions If someone else can stand a quarter circle away from the worker and watch the bit, that is the best help; otherwise, the worker himself must hold the brace steady while he walks around a quarter circle and judges whether the bit is straight. Care should be taken to hold the work level in the vise.

NAILS.

The words, "nail," "brad," and "nailing" are used somewhat interchangeably in this book; "nailing" may mean driving a brad. Brads have smaller, thicker heads, nails have larger, flat heads.

To drive a nail straight, start it straight. The hole cannot be straightened by bending the nail so that it looks straight after it is partly driven. Many gentle blows with the *hammer* will often drive a nail where heavy blows would fail. The fingers pinching the nail often prevent its bending. If possible, keep nails away from the corners of boards. Several nails joining two boards hold them stronger if the nails are driven at different angles. Nails are usually "set," that is, the heads are driven with a *nail-set* below the surface. They must always be set below surfaces which are to be planed. It is often wise not to drive the first nail or two way in until the work is examined. In withdrawing nails, a block under the hammer will often aid greatly, and also protect the surface of the work.

SCREWS.

Screws usually need holes properly bored to receive them; a large hole first, the size of the screw above the threads, a small hole next, the size at the roots of the threads (in hard wood somewhat larger), and a place for the head made with a *counter-sink*. Usually the screw should slip easily thru the first piece of wood and be tight in the second. The *screwdriver* should always be held in the line that the screw is going, and it ought fairly to fit the slot in the head. In hard wood, one must be careful not to twist screws off, especially brass screws, which are easily broken.

GLUE.

A beginner often wonders why things stick to his fingers instead of to their proper places; it is because he has a little glue on his fingers and usually a lot on the article; therefore, don't use too much glue. It is best, especially in holes and their pegs, to put glue on both surfaces of contact. Good glue will hold two surfaces, making good contact, stronger than the wood. Wipe off excess glue as soon as possible, using hot water for hot glue. Much labor is thus saved. Allow glue plenty of time to become dry. The moisture has to work its way thru the wood itself, and this takes hours; six to ten hours is not too long.

SANDPAPER.

Sandpaper varies in coarseness from No. 00 to No. 3, every sheet being stamped. It should not be used on a given piece until all work with edge tools is finished. The particles of sand left in the surface would quickly dull an edge tool. When using sandpaper on flat surfaces, wrap it closely about a rectangular block of wood. Try to keep all corners as sharp as they are left by the edge tools so that there will be a crispness of appearance which always marks good workmanship. Often the same care in holding work while sandpapering it must be taken as was taken when shaping it. Always sandpaper with, or lengthwise the grain.

DOWELS.

Sticks that are planed nearly to size can be made round and smooth by driving them thru a hole in a block of hard wood or iron; such sticks are called dowels. Two holes may be used if the second is only a little smaller than the first. Drive gently with a *mallet* rather than with a hammer. In many of the models in this book such dowels are used. Dowels (made by a different process, however,) can often be bought at hardware stores.

DRILLS.

For ease in making small holes, a *hand-drill* is essential. For some holes a headless nail will answer. To make better drills, break a needle, a knitting-needle, umbrella rib, or other piece of hard wire to suitable length; on a grindstone, flatten it near the point on two sides; then, putting it in the chuck of the hand-drill, try to hold it on the grindstone at the proper angle to form the two cutting edges; or it may be held against the edge of the bench and sharpened with an oilstone resting on top of the bench. Very convenient long drills can be thus made of knitting-needles.

SHARPENING.

To work with dull tools is altogether unsatisfactory. A boy should learn to sharpen his own edge tools. To grind a good bevel on a tool like a chisel, it must rest upon something steady. The reflection of light on the newly ground surface will indicate whether the surface is flat or not. This process of grinding makes what is called a feather-edge, or wire-edge, and the tool must be whetted on an oilstone to remove this wire-edge. The flat side *must be kept flat* on the stone; the bevel may be lifted just a trifle. When whetting the bevel, try to avoid a rocking motion, for this would round the edge. After the wire-edge is completely removed, a still keener edge can be obtained by stropping the tool on a piece of leather, much as a razor is stropped. A piece of leather glued to a wooden mount and sprinkled occasionally with the finest emery powder will help much in keeping the edge tools keen.

HOLDING WORK.

The way work is held in the vise often makes the difference between success and failure. Small surfaces are easily planed true if held almost flush with the jaws of the vise so that the top of the bench serves to guide the plane; for example, the wheel-center, page 20, or the crank, Plate 33, are easily planed in this manner. Sometimes articles, like spools, can be held endwise with safety when they might be crushed if squeezed sidewise.

A good way to hold the paddles of the sand wheel, Plate 21, Fig. 4, to saw the lines A B is to put the paddles about half-way down the end of the vise so that the back-saw can be held near the end of the vise jaws.

The *bench-hook* is the best device for holding a great deal of small work for sawing and for planing sides, corners, and ends. When planing ends, to avoid splitting the far corner, another piece of equal thickness may be put behind the first. The better way, however, is never to plane over the far corner, but turn the work and plane always towards the center; in other words, plane half way from each edge. Where a corner can be whittled off to form a buttress, there is practically no danger of splitting that corner. For planing thin boards, see page 19.

DIRECTIONS FOR PLANING.

1. Plane one broad surface. Test it *crosswise, lengthwise,* and *cornerwise.* This surface is called the *working-face,* and should be marked with a pencil line near the edge to be planed next. On a short board the cornerwise test can be made with a straight-edge; on a long board winding-sticks are needed. These are straight sticks with parallel edges. Near the ends of the board, stand them on edge across the board. With the eye some distance away, sight from one stick to the other, if one end of the farther stick seems elevated, that corner of the board must be planed more.

2. Plane one edge. Test it *crosswise* with the trysquare on the working-face, and *lengthwise* with a straight-edge. This is called the *working-edge.* Mark it with two pencil lines, drawn near the line on the working-face.

These two surfaces are of great importance. From them all measurements are made and all tests applied. The trysquare and the gage should always be kept on one of these two surfaces.

3. Square the ends. With the trysquare, test them from both the working-face and the working-edge.

4. Gage the width from the working-edge. Plane to the line. With the trysquare on the working-face, test this edge.

5. Gage the thickness from the working-face. Plane to the line.

Sometimes, of course, the above order needs to be changed. It is well to think out the best order of work.

Taking Aim

PROBLEMS

PLATES AND WORKING DIRECTIONS

DART—Plate 1.

A dart like the first one shown on Plate 1 will stick into a soft wooden target. Two or more boys, each with three darts, might have a contest in making the highest score. Number three rings of a target 5, 10, and 15, and the bull's eye 25.

The dart consists of two parts, a round stick and a paper rudder. To make the round stick, 7" long ¼" diameter, it will be well to start with a stick about 9" long so as to be able to hold it easily while planing it round. First plane the stick *square, ¼"*, and straight. To plane such a small stick straight, it should be laid on the top of the bench. While planing it, test it frequently by looking at it endwise. When it is the right size, grasp one end with the left hand, lay it on the bench with the forefinger touching the bench, and, with a small plane, plane away the corners so as to make a true octagonal (eight sided) stick. Next make it sixteen sided, taking very fine shavings, then sandpaper it well. Saw off the extra length, leaving the best part of the stick 7" long.

Bind one end with fine (screen) wire. To bind it well, make a square corner 1" from one end of the wire and lay this 1" lengthwise the stick. Hold it firmly with the left thumb while winding the long part of the wire smoothly around the stick and wire. Twist the two ends together, and cut off what is not needed. Gently pound down smooth the end of the wire that is left.

In this end of the stick, drill a hole for a 1" brad. File the head entirely off, and drive the brad in backwards, leaving 3/16" out; then file the point real sharp. Carefully split the other end of the stick 1". To do this, stand it upright in the vise, place a knife on the end, and tap the knife with a hammer. Into this split, insert the paper rudder bent as shown in Plate 1. The rudder should be cut the shape and size shown in the working drawing and then bent into shape.

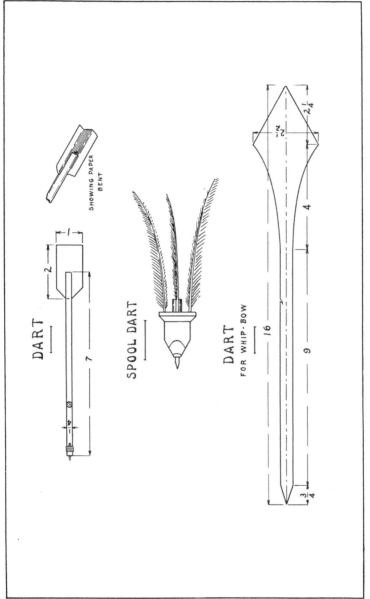

DART

SHOWING PAPER
BENT

SPOOL DART

DART
FOR WHIP-BOW

PLATE 1

SPOOL DART—PLATE 1.

An easier dart to throw can be made of a spool as shown on Plate 1. Three feathers which curve the same way will give the dart a whirling motion when it is thrown.

Make a stick about 7″ long to fit tightly into the hole of a spool about 1″ in diameter at its end. (See Dowels, page 11, also Glue, page 10.) A stick like this can be forced into a hole quite far by screwing it around, but if it is driven much with a hammer the spool will split easily. After the stick is glued into the spool, hold the spool upright on the jaws of the vise, and squeeze the stick extending below; then with the back-saw make four slanting cuts to sharpen the spool. File a 2¼″ nail square off, 1″ long; drive it backwards into a suitable hole drilled for it in the center of the spool; and sharpen it well with a file. One-half inch from the other end of the spool saw the stick off, and drill three holes in the spool end, into which glue three feathers about 4″ long.

DART FOR WHIP-BOW. PLATE 1.

This dart is best made of a shingle. Lacking that, plane a ½″ board thin* at one end to ⅛″. Draw the center line lengthwise and lay out the shape of the dart with the broad part at the thin end. Saw crosswise from each edge of the shingle to the place where the curve begins, then lengthwise to that point. Holding the thin end in the vise, pare the curves with a knife, spokeshave, or draw-knife. Make the point at each end with a plane. To plane to slanting lines such as these, it is very important to place the work in the vise at such a slant that the line is parallel with the top of the bench and quite close to the jaws of the vise. Find the point where the dart balances by testing it on the finger, and make the little notch for the string, using a back-saw first, then a knife.

A whip-bow consists of a string 20″ long tied to the end of a stick 20″ long. A knot is tied at the free end of the string. To throw the dart, catch the string in the notch, hold the wide end of the dart in the left hand and the stick in the right, throw the right hand forward, and let the dart fly from the string.

---

*To hold a board while planing it very thin, fasten it to another flat board with four wooden pegs.

For several of the models in this book, a flat board about 9″x4″x⅞″ with a cleat nailed to one end and extending ⅛″ above its upper surface will be found most convenient for holding thin boards while planing. If the cleat is a little wider than the height of the block on the bench-hook, the bench-hook serves well to hold it.

BUZZER—PLATE 2.

The buzzer consists of a wheel and two handles, connected with string. To make the wheel draw a 3″ circle on a piece of wood 3/16″ thick. Draw a line thru the center the way the grain goes and another at right angles to it, thus dividing the circle into quarters, Fig. 1. Notice, now, that to avoid splitting the circle, the four quarters must each be cut in a different direction. Lay the model flat on the bench-hook and saw off the corners of the square. Now, hold-

Fig. 1

ing it in the vise with one quarter up, with the spokeshave, pare the corners in the direction of the arrow in this quarter until the circle is reached. Be careful not to pare away any part of the line. It will be observed that paring can be done safely on the end grain beyond the arrow-head in this quarter, but this is not at all possible on the side grain where the arrow begins. The spokeshave should be held rather lightly so as to allow it to follow the curve. Observing carefully the direction of the arrows, proceed with the other quarters in this same manner. The last few chips should be very fine ones. Drill two small holes for the string ¼″ each side of the center. Sandpaper the model nicely. (See Sandpaper, page 11.)

The two handles can be planed best if held in the bench-hook and the plane turned with its side on the top of the bench. After the corners are planed in this way, the ends can be planed without danger of splitting. Drill the holes for the string. The edges and ends of the handles will look better not sandpapered.

String the model by passing one end of a 3 ft. string thru a hole in one handle, then in the wheel, then in the other handle, then back thru the other holes, tying it to the other end of the string. To make it go, take one handle in each hand, swing the wheel over and over, and gently pull the handles apart for an instant. A little practice may be necessary to make it go well. To make it buzz louder, bore two 5/16″ holes on opposite parts of the wheel ½″ from the rim. (See Bits, page 9.) To avoid splitting, bore *backwards* till the bit marks a deep circle in the wood.

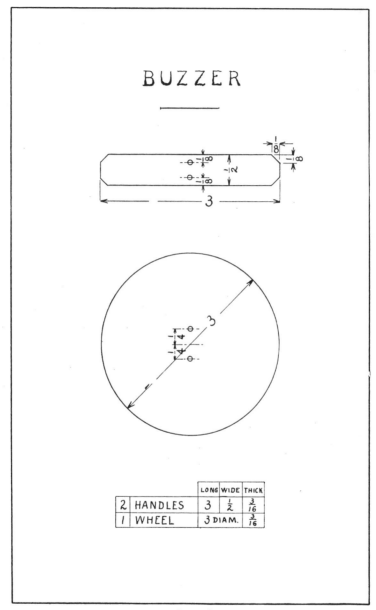

BUZZER

		LONG	WIDE	THICK
2	HANDLES	3	$\frac{1}{2}$	$\frac{3}{16}$
1	WHEEL	3 DIAM.		$\frac{3}{16}$

PLATE 2

FLYING TOP—Plate 3.

Like anything that flies, this top should be made as light as possible. Bass, cotton-wood, or soft pine are good woods to use. After the wood for the top is planed to size, a 3/16" hole should be bored straight thru the center. (See Bits, page 9.) Make the drawing on the top and whittle to line. Considerable care must be taken in whittling not to whittle away the two corners which should be saved; this is especially true if the grain is not straight. See page 16 for suggestions about making the handle. Glue the handle in the top. To make it fly, hold it between the two hands, and push the right one quickly. (See Plate 3.)

FLYING TOP—*(See Page 25)*

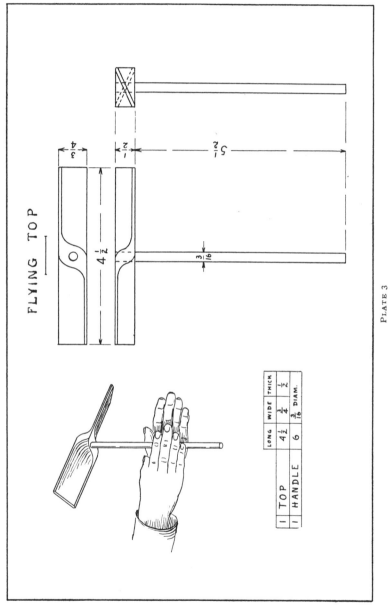

FLYING TOP

		LONG	WIDE	THICK
1	TOP	$4\frac{1}{2}$	$\frac{3}{4}$	$\frac{1}{2}$
1	HANDLE	6	$\frac{3}{16}$ DIAM.	

PLATE 3

FLYING TOP—Plate 4.

This form of flying top requires accurate work to make a good joint. (See Directions for Planing, page 13.) After planing the two vanes to size, the joint must be laid out with knife and gage lines and cut out with back-saw and chisel. Two important facts should be learned: The *length* of one notch equals the *width* of the other piece; the lines marking the depth of the notches must be gaged from the working-face of each piece. After the joint is laid out, hold the work in the bench-hook while sawing the depth of the notch, and be sure to saw *in the notch,* not outside the line. With a chisel held flat side down, pare between the saw cuts from each side of the wood towards the middle. When the joint is fitted, lay out the curves on each arm of the wheel, remembering that it is always the front corner of the right-hand arm, as the wheel turns around, that is to be whittled away. When all these curves are drawn, take the joint apart, and whittle to the lines. Glue the joint next, and bore a 3/16″ hole straight thru its center. Make the axle of hard wood. (See page 16 and Dowels, page 11.) Perhaps a skewer can be used.

After the handle is planed to size, draw pencil lines ¼″ from each edge for the chamfers. The curve of the chamfer may be drawn freehand. It should end 1 1/16″ from one end of the handle. A good chamfer is flat crosswise. If the grain of the wood is straight, the chamfers can be whittled easily; if it is crooked watch that it does not split over the line. After the chamfers are made, pare another one ⅛″ wide around the end of the handle. After the two blocks are planed, bore a ¼″ hole ⅜″ from one end. Glue and nail them 1″ on the handle.

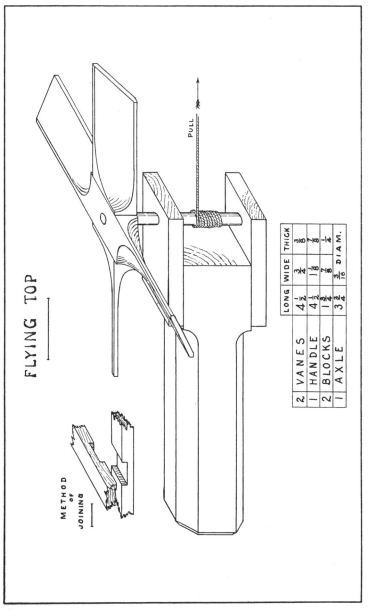

FLYING TOP

PULL

METHOD OF JOINING

		LONG	WIDE	THICK
2	VANES	$4\frac{1}{2}$	$\frac{3}{4}$	$\frac{3}{8}$
1	HANDLE	$4\frac{1}{2}$	$1\frac{1}{8}$	$\frac{7}{8}$
2	BLOCKS	$1\frac{3}{4}$	$\frac{7}{8}$	$\frac{1}{4}$
1	AXLE	$3\frac{3}{4}$	$\frac{3}{16}$ DIAM.	

PLATE 4

TOP—PLATE 5.

A variety of sizes, shapes and colors of tops, spinning on a plate, is a lively sight. The one suggested is perhaps as large as it should be made for such sport. Smaller ones are easily made of spools without making a disk, or wheel, for them. The more slender the spindle is, the faster one can spin the top. First make a stick about 6″ long to fit the hole in the spool. Plane 1″ of it tapering as small as ⅛″, then glue the spool on 1¼″ below this small end. Now hold the spool in the vise endwise, and make, with the back-saw, a saw cut half thru the spool on the same slant as the slanting part of the spool; then saw straight down to the end of this slanting cut. Turn the spool nearly over and repeat this operation; then saw it completely off, and whittle the spool to a good point.

Draw a 2″ circle on a piece of wood ¼″ thick. Draw other circles just as desired for coloring. Observe the directions on page 20 for making a wheel. When the wheel is round, bore a 5/16″ hole in its center, sandpaper it, and glue it in place on the spool and spindle. It can be colored with crayons or water colors.

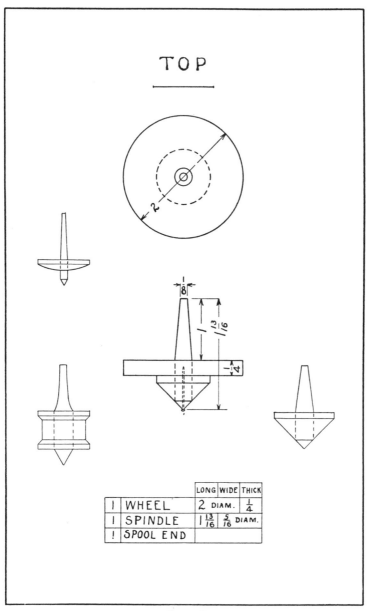

TOP

		LONG	WIDE	THICK
1	WHEEL	2 DIAM.		$\frac{1}{4}$
1	SPINDLE	$1\frac{13}{16}$	$\frac{5}{16}$ DIAM.	
1	SPOOL END			

PLATE 5

TOM-TOM DRUM—Plate 6.

As in a violin, the sounding qualities of this drum depend upon the quality of the wood used and the thickness of the sounding-board. Spruce is a good wood to use, though the drum-stick may well be harder.

A good way to make two pieces the same length and thickness is to plane *one* piece, which is wider than the two pieces combined, to the right length and thickness, and then saw it in two lengthwise; so, to make the top and between pieces it will be best to start with one piece about 6"x⅞"x5/16". If no wood ⅛" thick for the sounding-boards is at hand, plane a thicker piece nicely on all surfaces 3"x2"x5/16". Then gage a line ⅛" from each broad surface all around the piece and saw between these lines. To plane these two pieces, lay them on the board described in the foot-note on page 19.

Glue and nail the parts together with very small brads, or pins cut off ½". Allow the glue to dry six to ten hours before twisting the drumstick in the strings. Cut a small notch near the ends of the top pieces in which to wind two or three strands of string. Twist the drumstick in the opposite way from which it should strike the sounding-board. To play it, hold it in the left hand, and let the fingers of the right hand slide over the end of the drum-stick, thus making the drum-stick strike the sounding-board.

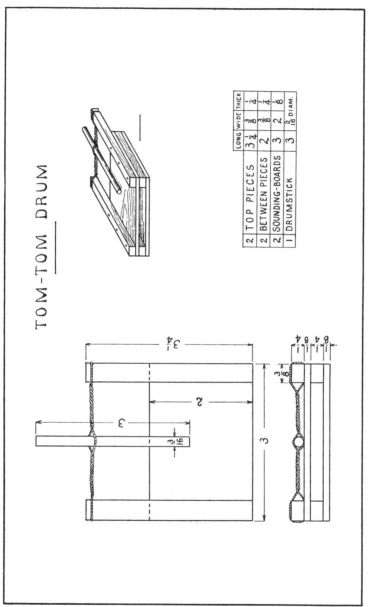

TOM-TOM DRUM

		LONG	WIDE	THICK
2	TOP PIECES	$3\frac{1}{4}$	$\frac{3}{8}$	$\frac{1}{4}$
2	BETWEEN PIECES	2	$\frac{3}{8}$	$\frac{1}{4}$
2	SOUNDING-BOARDS	3	2	$\frac{1}{8}$
1	DRUMSTICK	3	$\frac{3}{16}$ DIAM.	

PLATE 6

POP-GUN—Plate 7.

The part of this model difficult to make is a nice, smooth hole. The surest way is to start with a thick piece of wood for the barrel, 6"x1¼"x1¼". Draw a ⅞" circle on one end; then bore the 7/16" hole as straight as possible, starting at the center of the circle. Stop boring as soon as the spur of the bit pricks thru the other end, and draw another ⅞" circle, setting the needle-point of the compass in the tiny hole made by the spur; then finish boring. Next plane the piece round the size of the circles. The ramrod should be made as directed on page 16. The hole should now be sandpapered by wrapping a long, narrow piece of sandpaper snugly about the ramrod, and tying it securely at each end with string. Make the handle, being careful to bore the hole straight 1" deep, and glue the ramrod into it.

Cut off ⅜" of that part of a cork which fits tightly in the barrel. Drive a slender nail or brad thru a piece of hard leather (or zinc or copper) and trim it round ¼" diameter. Drill a small hole exactly in the center of the end of the ramrod, then drive the nail thru the center of the cork and into the ramrod.

To make the hole in the barrel still better, let a few drippings from a candle fall into it and quickly insert the ramrod and push it back and forth rapidly. A sudden push of the ramrod will blow the other cork out with a loud pop. To keep this cork, tie one end of a string around it and the other end around the barrel.

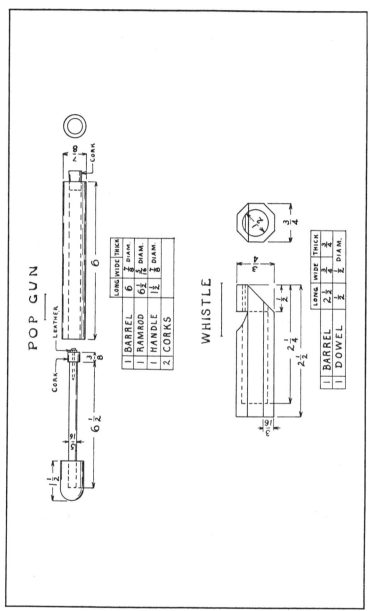

POP GUN

	LONG	WIDE	THICK
1 BARREL	6	$\frac{7}{8}$ DIAM.	
1 RAMROD	$6\frac{1}{2}$	$\frac{5}{16}$ DIAM.	
1 HANDLE	$1\frac{1}{2}$	$\frac{7}{8}$ DIAM.	
2 CORKS			

WHISTLE

	LONG	WIDE	THICK
1 BARREL	$2\frac{1}{2}$	$\frac{3}{4}$	$\frac{3}{4}$
1 DOWEL	$\frac{1}{2}$	$\frac{1}{2}$ DIAM.	

PLATE 7

—3

WHISTLE—PLATE 7.

The size of the chamber, of the notch, of the inlet for air, the force with which air is blown in,—these are some of the conditions which affect the tone of a whistle.

Plane a piece of close-grained wood 6"x¾"x¾". This length is suggested so that two trials at boring can be made. Bore a ½" hole 2¼" deep. To help in boring this straight, clamp a straight-edge (the ruler may do) in the vise together with the square stick. Have one edge of the straight-edge on the center of one side of the stick. After boring a straight hole, draw pencil lines 3/16" from the long edges on all four sides. A good way to draw such lines is to rest the middle finger-nail on a side of the stick as a guide and hold the pencil closely over this nail while sliding it along. The hand must be held rather rigid. Practice will enable one to draw lines quite accurately this way. Place the stick in the vise so that one edge is straight up, and plane the corner off to the line. Plane all four corners so as to make a good octagonal stick. Make a dowel (see page 11) about 1½" long to fit nicely in the hole. Do not crowd it so hard as to split the whistle. It might well be fitted first in a ½" hole bored in a waste piece of wood. Plane off a side of this dowel till a flat place is made ⅜" wide. Push the dowel into the whistle and saw the straight end of the notch about 3/16" deep. Pare the rest of the notch with knife or chisel, testing the whistle by blowing it occasionally as the paring proceeds. When it sounds best, glue the dowel in place and allow it to dry before sawing it off and cutting the slanting part. When this is done saw the whistle to a length of 2½". If a rolling sound is desired, put in a pea before gluing the dowel in place.

ARROW—Plate 8.

The old saying, "Straight as an arrow," suggests an arrow's most important quality: it must be straight. Saw a strip 20"x½" from the edge of a straight-grained spruce board and plane it according to directions on page 16. To make the notch for the bow-string, first file a notch in the smaller end, then saw it ¼" deep, and smooth it with the folded edge of a piece of sandpaper. Bind the larger end tightly with rather small, soft wire. (See page 16.) Pigeon feathers are easiest to use because the quills are soft and straight. Turkey and goose feathers are good, and hen feathers will do if they are nearly straight. The quill should be split with the point of a small, sharp knife, the feather being held on a cutting board. About 3" of quill are needed. With scissors, trim the feather about 5/16" wide; then glue and pin it in place 1¼" from the smaller end of the arrow. Indians use three feathers, but two will do for a boy. When the feathers are in place, the ends of the quills must be bound very smoothly and tightly with thread. Notice the position of the feathers in Plate 8: the *bottom* feather on the arrow having three feathers is called the cock-feather and should be of a different color from the other two. It is always placed on the bowstring *away* from the bow.

BOW—Plate 8.

Almost any tough stick that will bend to a good curve will answer for a bow, but white ash such as is used in hoe- and rake-handles is probably best and easiest to get. A brittle wood like hemlock can be used, if used with great care; indeed, some Eskimos, who can get only dry, brittle driftwood, still make a splendid bow by wrapping it completely with sinew. The bow should be shorter than the archer. Plane each end tapering, first on the bottom, then on the two edges. Leave 6″ in the middle straight for a handle. Notice the shape,

Timber-hitch knot   Fig. 2   Bowline-knot

Plate 8, of the three steps in the planing of the bow. Be especially careful to get the second step right, then the third will come easily. File notches near each end somewhat the shape of the loop on the bowstring. Before the bow can be finished, it must be strung and pulled a little to test it,—to see if both ends bend the same good curve,—not the curve of a circle, but that of the broad side of an ellipse. The ends should curve more than the middle. When it bends true, smooth it well with a coarse file, or glass, and sandpaper. Do not be tempted to pull the bow too far and so break it; one that bends easily is less apt to break than one that is too strong. When the bow is strung, the center of it and of the bowstring should be marked with thread or color.

A piece of strong fish-line makes a good bowstring. A good one can be made of linen thread on the string machine shown on Plate 34. Tie knots as shown in Fig. 2. The timber-hitch should be kept in place on the bow, and the bowline-knot slipped back on the bow when it is unstrung. The best way to string a bow is to place the end having the timber-hitch on the ground against one's left foot, then to pull the middle of the bow with the left hand, and to push the upper part with the right hand, allowing this hand to slide upward so as to shove the bowline-knot into the upper notch. When finished the bow can be improved by rubbing it well with grease.

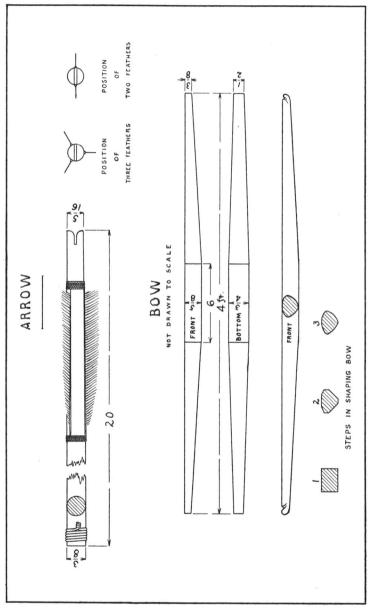

ARROW

POSITION OF TWO FEATHERS

POSITION OF THREE FEATHERS

BOW

NOT DRAWN TO SCALE

STEPS IN SHAPING BOW

PLATE 8

SWORD—Plate 9.

Plane the blade to size, then draw a center line on each side, and lay out the curves for the point and handle. Shape these ends with the draw-knife, spokeshave, or block-plane. Now measure 5″ for the handle, and draw a line along the center of each edge to mark the cutting edges of the sword. A workman would do this with his pencil resting over his finger-nail as mentioned on page 32. Use the spokeshave to pare off the four corners (to sharpen the sword), and finish them with a plane. Try to take broad, flat chips so as to make the blade a good diamond shape. Where the blade and handle meet a good square shoulder must be made. A boy can do this best, perhaps, with a wide, flat file, though a workman would use a back-saw and chisel.

Saw out the guard 5″x3″x$\frac{1}{2}$″; then draw the diamond 1$\frac{1}{2}$‴ long and $\frac{1}{2}$″ wide. It is not easy for a boy to cut this out, so be careful and guard against splitting the board. First drill small holes at each end of the diamond, then bore other holes as large as will go within the diamond, Plate 9. With a thin chisel pare straight thru the board onto a cutting board. When the diamond will fit the blade, draw the shape of the guard freehand and pare the edges as explained for the buzzer on page 20. Sandpaper both parts of the sword, and fasten the guard with glue and two 2″ brads, driven from each edge of the guard in holes drilled for the purpose.

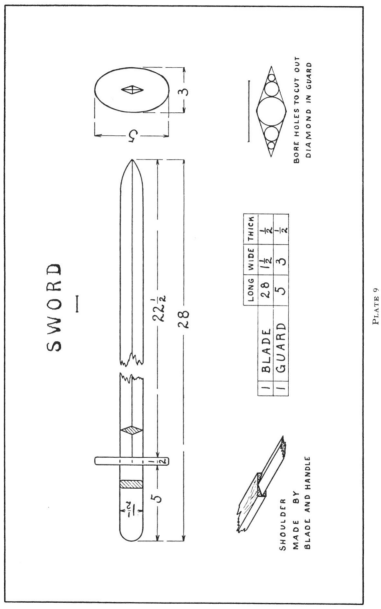

SWORD

		LONG	WIDE	THICK
1	BLADE	28	$1\frac{1}{2}$	$\frac{1}{2}$
1	GUARD	5	3	$\frac{1}{2}$

BORE HOLES TO CUT OUT
DIAMOND IN GUARD

SHOULDER
MADE BY
BLADE AND HANDLE

PLATE 9

MAGIC BOX—PLATE 10.

This is truly a magic box to those who do not understand how it works. Who would ever think that these little bits of people would hop up and down inside their house just because their window was rubbed with a piece of leather? Try it and see how excited they get.

If the worker can cut glass, make the box first, otherwise he must get a piece of glass 5½"x3" and build the box to fit it. It requires careful work to make a good box, so be sure that all ends and edges are square and that corresponding parts are the same size before nailing it together. Plane all such small boards in the bench-hook. Make the ends first 1" wide and as *long* as the glass is *wide*. Make the sides the same width and as long as the glass, *plus* the thickness of the two ends. Glue and nail these to the ends, keeping the bottom edges flush. Set all nails with a nail-set.

One edge and one end only of the bottom should now be planed square, the other edge and end being left to plane after the bottom is nailed in place. Cut a piece of tin 1/16" smaller than the glass, or glue some tinfoil on the inside of the bottom. If tinfoil is to be used, smooth it on a piece of paper carefully with the fingers; then spread some glue thinly over the bottom, and lay the tinfoil on it. The squared edge and end of the bottom are to be nailed first, having them fit nicely; then the other edge and end. Never drive a nail too near the corner of the bottom lest it strike the nails driven thru the sides of the box. Now plane the end and then the side of the bottom to fit. If tin is used instead of tinfoil put it inside the box after the bottom has been nailed in place. Make the two supports fit inside the box lengthwise and just wide enough to hold the top of the glass flush with the top edges of the box. To hold the supports, drive nails thru the ends of the box into them.

Everything about electrical apparatus should be clean and dry, so, as this is really an electric box, have the glass and tin clean before using it. Put some bits of charcoal, paper, straw, or sawdust into the box, have it warm and dry, rub the glass with a piece of leather (glove, shoe), and then see how the little people jump! The ex-

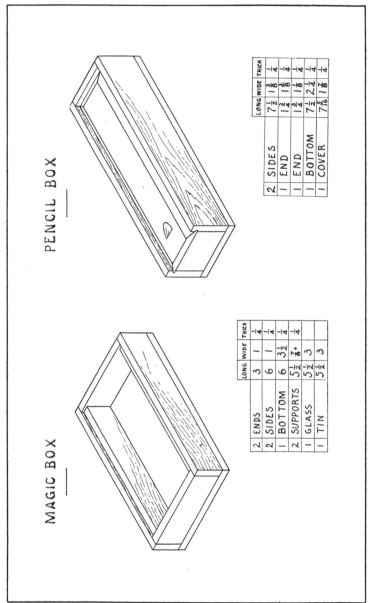

PENCIL BOX

		LONG	WIDE	THICK
2	SIDES	$7\frac{1}{2}$	3	$\frac{1}{4}$
1	END	$1\frac{3}{4}$	$1\frac{1}{8}$	$\frac{1}{4}$
1	END	$1\frac{3}{4}$	$1\frac{1}{8}$	$\frac{1}{4}$
1	BOTTOM	$7\frac{1}{2}$	$2\frac{1}{4}$	$\frac{1}{4}$
1	COVER	$7\frac{5}{16}$	$1\frac{7}{8}$	$\frac{1}{4}$

MAGIC BOX

		LONG	WIDE	THICK
2	ENDS	3	1	$\frac{1}{4}$
2	SIDES	6	1	$\frac{1}{4}$
1	BOTTOM	6	$3\frac{1}{2}$	$\frac{1}{4}$
2	SUPPORTS	$5\frac{1}{2}$	$\frac{7}{8}+$	$\frac{1}{4}$
1	GLASS	$5\frac{1}{2}$	3	
1	TIN	$5\frac{1}{2}$	3	

PLATE 10

planation is as follows: Rubbing glass with leather, fur, woolen, or silk *generates* electricity; this electricity *attracts* non-electrified bodies, thus lifting the little people to the glass; as soon as they become *charged* with the electricity on the glass, they are *repelled* and thrown down to the tin; the tin *conducts* their charge of electricity away, and they are ready to begin their circus over again.

PENCIL-BOX—Plate 10.

To make this box, saw out one long piece for the sides and ends, 22"x1⅞"x¼", or two shorter pieces, 12"x1⅞"x¼". The reason for having them so long is because it is difficult to make the groove nicely to the end of the board; and they are wide enough to try twice to make the groove.

File a nail (about 3/32" in diameter) sharp like a chisel, and drive it tightly into a small hole, drilled in a block of wood which

Fig. 3

has one corner rabbeted, that is, sawed away as shown in Fig. 3. The outside of the nail, measured from the shoulder of the rabbet, must be exactly ¼" away, so that the lower edge of the groove will be ¼" from the top of the box. Practice with this tool till a good groove can be made in waste lumber, then make the groove along one edge of the board. When well done, plane the board 1⅜" wide, and saw it to the proper lengths for sides and ends. In the front end there is no groove, so plane it away from one piece just sawed. Sandpaper the flat sides before gluing and nailing them together. Prepare the bottom as directed for the magic box, page 38, then sandpaper, glue and nail it in place. Set all nails. Plane the bottom to fit. Prepare the cover somewhat too long but exactly the width between the grooves. As in making the whistle, page 32, so here draw pencil lines for the bevel ⅜" wide on the cover. Practice planing a bevel on waste wood first. The bevel at the further end of the cover can be planed by holding the cover upright in the vise. When it slides smoothly in the grooves, saw it the right length. For the notch, make a deep cut with a gouge, and cut the chip straight across with knife point or small chisel. Hold it in the bench-hook while doing this.

TELEPHONE—Plate 11.

In these days when even boys are using wireless telegraphy, this may seem a humble telephone, but it is a surprisingly good one, and it is very easily made and operated. The drum should be hard and tight, the string should be a small, hard cord (tho the common pink cord thoroly waxed with paraffin will do), and the cord should be supported by nothing but the drums when the telephone is being used.

After preparing the eight sides, observe in Plate 11, the method of nailing four boards of equal width together to form a square,—each one is nailed to another one. The ends of the boxes should be well rounded with sandpaper before the drum is stretched over them.

The best material for the drum is rawhide,—the dried skin of an animal. The skin of a small animal like the cat, rabbit, or woodchuck is best. Country boys will not have much difficulty in securing such rawhide, but city boys may. To remove the hair, or fur, from a skin, slack a lump of lime as large as a hen's egg in a basin of water and soak the skin in it until the hair can be pulled off readily (usually a few minutes); then thoroly wash the skin, stretch it over one end of a box, and tack it every $\frac{3}{8}''$ with 2 oz. tacks. When thoroly dry it will be "tight as a drum" and ready to use. A good drum can also be made of an old (dressed) kid glove or shoe. Soak a piece 4" sq. in water a few minutes then stretch it while still wet, tightly over the box. When dry, coat it on both sides with melted paraffin. Fasten the cord to the drum simply by a knot on the inside. If common pink cord is used, drive the paraffin in with a hot flat-iron.

To use the telephone, a boy at each end of the line holds his box so that the string will not touch anything, then one talks into his box while the other listens in his. The telephone may be stretched from one house to another if the houses are within several hundred feet of each other and have a free space between. If two telephones were provided, a person could talk and listen at the same time.

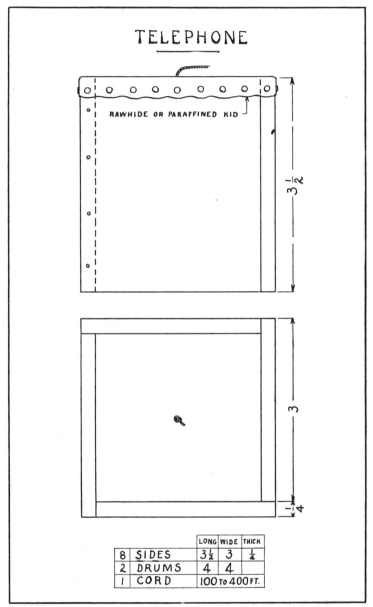

TELEPHONE

RAWHIDE OR PARAFFINED KID

$3\frac{1}{2}$

3

$\frac{1}{4}$

		LONG	WIDE	THICK
8	SIDES	$3\frac{1}{2}$	3	$\frac{1}{4}$
2	DRUMS	4	4	
1	CORD	100 TO 400 FT.		

PLATE 11

HAPPY JACK WINDMILL.—PLATE 12.

On a windy day "Happy Jack" will be a whole circus out on the clothes-line post. If he can be painted in bright colors so much the better, otherwise he should be decorated with colored pencils.

The body is drawn on a board, 9"x2"x½", by measuring all the figures from the hat down, and at these points drawing lines square across the board; also, draw a center-line from head to heel. The toes and hat rim split easily, so be careful of these parts. If no scroll-saw is at hand, saw every ⅜" with the back-saw straight across from the edge of the board to the outline of the body; then pare these little pieces away with a knife or chisel. The curves at the neck are best made with a No. 6 bit before sawing. The curves may be finished with half-round file or sandpaper. Take great care in boring the hole up the legs and across the shoulders; if a hole is started crooked, glue in a dowel of the same wood (see Dowels, page 11), let it dry, and then try again. Use a straight-edge as a guide, as for the whistle, page 32. A No. 3 bit is used thru the shoulders, and a No. 4 bit up the legs. To make the arms, use a ½" hard wood dowel 6" long. Bore ¼" holes for the vanes ½" each side the center of the dowel and file the wrists, before sawing it in two. Round the ends some with sandpaper. Flatten the 4" wire which goes thru the shoulders enough to keep it from turning in the arms. Drill holes in the arms to hold the wire firmly. To plane the vanes thin at the broad end, use the board mentioned at the bottom of page 19. When gluing and nailing the vanes in the arms, remember that one lies flat and the other nearly edgewise; also remember to make them balance. Bore a 3/16" hole in the center of the base and glue the dowel into it. Before trying to fasten "Happy Jack" to a post, drill holes in the base for nails or screws.

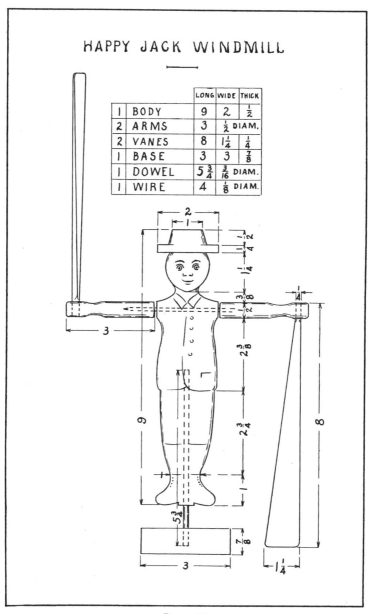

HAPPY JACK WINDMILL

		LONG	WIDE	THICK
1	BODY	9	2	$\frac{1}{2}$
2	ARMS	3	$\frac{1}{2}$ DIAM.	
2	VANES	8	$1\frac{1}{4}$	$\frac{1}{4}$
1	BASE	3	3	$\frac{7}{8}$
1	DOWEL	$5\frac{3}{4}$	$\frac{3}{16}$ DIAM.	
1	WIRE	4	$\frac{1}{8}$ DIAM.	

PLATE 12

GLOUCESTER "HAPPY JACK" WINDMILL—Plate 13.

This "Happy Jack" is the kind which is common along the coast of New England. He is often painted with blue and white uniform and black shoes, while the paddles are left unpainted.

The drawing is made on squares so that it may be enlarged easily to any size. Keep the same *number* of squares but make them any size desired; ¾″ is a good size. The hat, being made separate from the body, should not be drawn on the same board.

To make the hat without a lathe, make two wheels of soft wood, round one edge of the larger, and glue and nail the smaller one on it. Saw the head slanting to make a flat place for the hat, as shown in side view of hat, Plate 13. The space between the legs should be cut out with a turning or key-hole saw, tho it can be worked out as the diamond in the sword guard, Plate 9. The "Happy Jack" should be mounted on a large wire rod.

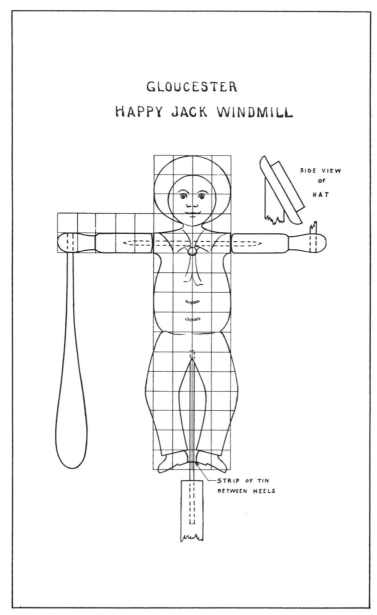

GLOUCESTER
HAPPY JACK WINDMILL

SIDE VIEW
OF
HAT

STRIP OF TIN
BETWEEN HEELS

PLATE 13

— 4

PADDLING INDIAN WINDMILL—Plate 14.

Make this windmill any dimension desired, using the same number of squares in drawing to keep the proportions. The stern of the canoe should be planed thin enough so that the completed windmill will nearly or quite balance on the upright wire rod. The arms should be made like those on the "Happy Jack," and as long as from the center of the shoulder to the topmost feather. If the canoe is not too wide, the Indian can be nailed in place by two nails as shown in Plate 14, otherwise drive smaller ones slanting thru the back into the canoe; drill holes in either case. After the hole is bored thru the shoulders, use a trysquare to tell where to start the hole up thru the canoe so that it shall come in front of the former.

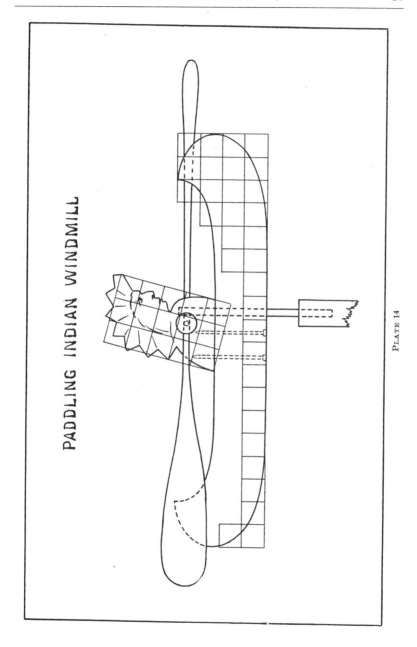

PADDLING INDIAN WINDMILL

PLATE 14

KITE—PLATE 15.

Kite flying is such fascinating sport that the three typical kites here given will make one want to build others, larger and of different shapes.* Kites have been made large enough to carry a man high in the air. The adjustments of a kite are so subtle that much patience is sometimes needed to make it fly. That is why the rather elaborate bridle is suggested for the paper covered kite with tail. It will require a little longer stay in the workshop, but it will save time outdoors.

To make the spine and crosspiece, saw a $\frac{1}{4}''$ strip from the edge of a $\frac{7}{8}''$ straight-grained spruce board 3 ft. long; then saw this strip again lengthwise, and plane the two pieces 3 ft.x$\frac{3}{8}''$x$\frac{1}{4}''$. Mark the center of the crosspiece and a point 8" from the top of the spine, and plane each end tapering thinner to 3/16". In each end saw a slot 3/16" deep, Plate 15. Glue and bind securely the middle of the crosspiece to the 8" point on the spine. Notice that the last few strands go *around* the others. Test the sticks to see that they are square with each other. This can be done by measuring from one end of the spine to each end of the crosspiece. Put a cord that will not stretch around the ends of the sticks, in the slots, and tie it tightly. Bind this cord into each slot in such a manner that it will not slip, and at the same time wind the sticks so that they will not split beyond the slot. While doing this, one must measure again from each end of the spine to the ends of the crosspiece so that the two halves of the kite will be equal.

Cover the kite with strong, light paper. Glue the paper to the sticks, and fold it over the string $\frac{1}{2}''$. Try to have the string lay in the crease of the fold. Strengthen the corners with another piece of paper, 2" wide.

To make an adjustable bridle, wind a cord twice around the spine near its top and tie it tightly on the front side, keeping the knot in the middle. Little holes will, of course, have to be made in the paper.

*Many suggestions are found in "The Construction and Flying of Kites" by Charles M. Miller, price 20 cents, Manual Arts Press, Peoria, Ill.

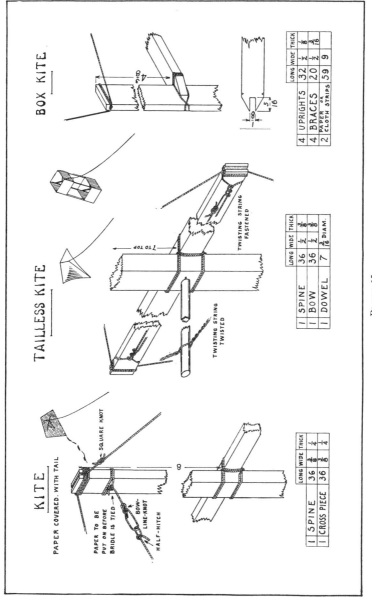

BOX KITE

	LONG	WIDE	THICK
4 UPRIGHTS	32	$\frac{1}{2}$	$\frac{1}{8}$
4 BRACES	20	$\frac{1}{2}$	$\frac{3}{16}$
2 PAPER or CLOTH STRIPS	59	9	

TAILLESS KITE

TWISTING STRING FASTENED

7 TO TOP

TWISTING STRING TWISTED

	LONG	WIDE	THICK
1 SPINE	36	$\frac{1}{2}$	$\frac{3}{8}$
1 BOW	36	$\frac{1}{2}$	$\frac{3}{8}$
1 DOWEL	7		$\frac{3}{16}$ DIAM.

KITE

PAPER COVERED. WITH TAIL

SQUARE KNOT

PAPER TO BE PUT ON BEFORE BRIDLE IS TIED

BOW-LINE-KNOT

HALF-HITCH

	LONG	WIDE	THICK
1 SPINE	36	$\frac{3}{8}$	$\frac{1}{4}$
1 CROSS PIECE	36	$\frac{3}{8}$	$\frac{1}{4}$

PLATE 15

Cut the cord about 2″ long and tie bowline-knot, Fig. 2, p. 34. Measure on the crosspiece 10″ from the center, and down the spine 12″ from the crosspiece, and tie three more such knots. Double two cords, about 40″ long, and tie them in one big knot, called the flying-knot, to make a loop about 1″ long to which to fasten the anchor line. Mark a point on the spine 10″ below the cross-piece. Hold the flying-knot here, and fasten two cords to the loops on the crosspiece with two or three half-hitches, Plate 15. Now bring the flying-knot 2″ above the crosspiece and out from the kite far enough to make these two cords taut. Fasten another cord to the loop at the upper part of the spine. Adjust the remaining cord as taut as the others.

A flat kite like this always needs a tail, and the most bothersome tail ever made is that familiar kind made of paper and string. To make a convenient, serviceable, and easily-made tail use strips, 3″ wide, of bunting, cheese-cloth, or any soft, light cloth.

In a high wind a longer tail is needed than in a light wind. If the kite seems too unsteady, pull it down, and try to adjust the bridle or the tail, before an accident occurs. If the kite dives, let go the string just before the kite reaches the ground so that it will not strike the ground with force enough to smash the kite. When let-ting out string rapidly, always protect the hand with a cloth or glove lest the string cut thru the skin. If in doubt about the strength of the anchor-line, two boys can very quickly test it 100 ft. or so at a time as it is being let out; one does not want the string to break when the kite is high in the air.

TAILLESS KITE—Plate 15.

If one has to fly a kite amid many obstructions of trees, wires, and houses, one will appreciate the advantage of a tailless kite. Such a kite has to be more accurately made, however, and should be covered with cloth.

When making the bow, file notches near the slot at each end in the same manner as for the bow, Plate 8, in which the twisting string will be fastened later. Lash the middle of the bow to a point 7″ from the top of the spine. In the slots, put the cord which goes around the kite, measuring carefully to keep the two sides the same size. Sew a piece of colored cambric over the kite. Tie the middle of a strong cord 6½ feet long to the filed notch at one end of the bow with three half-hitches, as shown in Plate 15. Pass one part of this cord around the other notch, and fasten it in the same manner; then tie the two ends together with a square knot. Make the dowel for twisting the two cords on the back of the bow so as to bend the bow as desired. Into one end of the dowel drive a small brad and file it sharp. How much to bend the bow can be determined only by trying the kite. As the bow bends, the cloth becomes looser, and it is this looseness of the cloth which so holds the wind that the kite will fly without a tail. After twisting the cords enough, slip them towards the end of the dowel away from the spur, and rest the spur in the back of the spine.

Tie a string around both the top and the bottom ends of the spine for the bridle. The flying-knot should come as far as the end of the bow; or, some tie the lower end of the bridle about 14″ from the lower end of the spine, and make the flying-knot about 9″ in front and 2″ above the bow.

BOX KITE—PLATE 15.

In a gale too strong for other kites, a box kite will fly safely. The bridle is very easy to adjust, and the kite, tho somewhat more elaborate than the others, is not difficult to make. Thin sticks like these can be sawed from the edge of a straight-grained board. An easy way to make the notches in the ends of the braces is to clamp them all in the vise at once, flat surfaces together, and then saw them out with a back-saw. This method presupposes that the uprights are all planed the same thickness. If they are unequal in thickness, saw the notches as wide as the thinnest upright and pare the others each to fit its proper upright. In any construction like this, which has a number of parts fitting together, it is well to number the adjacent parts so that they may be put together again, each in its place. Little nicks are cut with a knife on the four edges of the braces where the lashing is to be wound. When all the sticks are fitted together, glue the braces to the uprights $4\frac{3}{8}$" from the ends; two frames are thus made just alike. The lashing is done with large thread. Start it with two turns around the brace, then once around the upright, then once around the brace, then again around the upright, and so continue. The last few turns should be around the brace. See that the thread goes from the brace to the upright in the way most favorable for holding. When all the lashing is done, measure the center of each brace. Put one frame thru the other, and drive a pin thru the two centers. Now the frames must be brought to a $14\frac{1}{2}$" square by means of strong thread. Near the top of one upright tie a 6 ft. thread, leaving a short end. Simply wind the long end twice around each upright, and tie the end with a bow-knot until all sides of the square can be measured and adjusted. When all sides are equal, make the bow-knot into a square knot. Wind some thread around each upright, except the first, in such a manner as to hold the long thread securely. Now adjust the other end of the kite in the same way. Measure $8\frac{3}{4}$" from the ends of each upright and put other threads around the square. These can be fastened at each upright after the first by three half-hitches.

The kite may be covered either with cloth or paper. If cloth is used, the edges should be hemmed. If paper, lay it on the floor, put glue on each upright, then press the paper to one upright. Wrap the paper around the kite and wind string around it several times to hold it while adjusting and pressing each corner. Glue the ends of the paper next, pulling them as tight as possible. Two flat-irons will hold the ends while drying. After the paper is on, its edges should be strengthened with a narrow ribbon of cloth glued to it.

Tie the bridle strings just above and below the upper cell and have the flying-knot 5″ in front of the end of the brace.

BOX KITE AND KITE-STRING REEL

KITE-STRING SAILBOAT—Plate 16.

To send messages up to his kite, many a boy has made a hole in a piece of paper and watched that go sailing up his anchor line. This sailboat will do that, and other things too, and come spinning down again to take another message. A parachute, made of a paper napkin, having a 12″ thread running to each corner and a nail for ballast tied where the four threads are knotted together, can be sent up by this messenger, released, and allowed to float down from a great height. Paper gliders sent up this way will do many "stunts" before they reach ground. Fold a flimsy paper napkin in such a way as to hold a bunch of confetti with a pin thru only three or four thicknesses of the napkin. This can be tied to the keel and the pin withdrawn by the release and fall of a nail, and, behold, a shower of confetti! Be sure the falling nail will do no injury where it strikes. (See Frontispiece.)

A light, frail model like this will require considerable time and patience to make and adjust so that it will work. Make the hull and posts from a stick about 13″ long. Bore the 3/16″ holes for the mast and keel, the former a little to the left (port, a sailor would say) of the center and 2½″ from the bow, the latter in the center 2″ from the stern. Make the wheels of the ends of spools by sawing them off just where the straight portion begins, and glueing them together on a hard dowel. Very accurately find their centers and drill holes for 1″ brads which form their axles. Drive these into the post so that the wheels run very freely. Do not nail the posts to the hull till the wire parts have been put in place. Make three staples of pins and drive them in the bottom of the hull so that a fine wire will just slide thru them easily. Three are used so that the wire will always be held straight. Next make the two eyes which hold the kite-string under the wheels. Coiled around once and a half, the coils must be separated enough to allow the string to slip between. The safety of the model, swinging violently high in the air, depends upon these eyes. They can be driven thru small, tight holes and bent on the under side to make them secure. They must be just high enough to allow the string to run free. The forward

KITE-STRING SAILBOAT

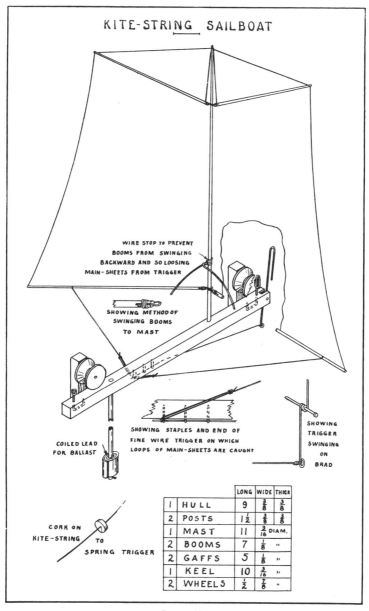

WIRE STOP TO PREVENT
BOOMS FROM SWINGING
BACKWARD AND SO LOOSING
MAIN-SHEETS FROM TRIGGER

SHOWING METHOD OF
SWINGING BOOMS
TO MAST

SHOWING STAPLES AND END OF
FINE WIRE TRIGGER ON WHICH
LOOPS OF MAIN-SHEETS ARE CAUGHT

COILED LEAD
FOR BALLAST

SHOWING
TRIGGER
SWINGING
ON
BRAD

CORK ON
KITE-STRING
TO
SPRING TRIGGER

		LONG	WIDE	THICK
1	HULL	9	$\frac{3}{8}$	$\frac{3}{8}$
2	POSTS	$1\frac{1}{2}$	$\frac{3}{8}$	$\frac{3}{8}$
1	MAST	11	$\frac{3}{16}$ DIAM.	
2	BOOMS	7	$\frac{1}{8}$	"
2	GAFFS	5	$\frac{1}{8}$	"
1	KEEL	10	$\frac{3}{16}$	"
2	WHEELS	$\frac{1}{2}$	$\frac{1}{8}$	"

PLATE 16

one is elongated because the kite-string slants upward so much. Bend the 4″ wire trigger three times around a brad driven in a piece of wood for convenience. To handle wire readily for such work as this, two pliers will be found useful. Saw a notch in the bow just wide enough for this coil. Now glue and nail the posts in position.

Make the mast, all the spars, in fact, smaller at the outer end. Rig it completely before gluing the mat in place. Be sure that the booms will swing *over* the forward wheel, so as not to interfere with its easy running. The sails should be of light cloth. The booms and the gaffs (see Plate 30 for names of parts) must swing freely on the mast, so as to fold together when the trigger is released. For the main-sheets, use thread tied with a long loop to slip over the fine wire part of the trigger. A cork $1\frac{1}{4}″$ in diameter, slit to the center, can be put on the kite-string far enough from the kite to be safe from any entangling. On the keel, fasten ballast enough (about 1 oz.) to make the sailboat ride upright.

THE HYGROSCOPE OR WEATHER COTTAGE—PLATE 17.

This model serves to indicate the humidity (dampness) of the air. It consists of the house, turntable, and figures, the turntable being suspended on a violin string. The violin string absorbs moisture from the air and untwists, thus causing the man to come out; when the air become dry the string twists tighter, thus causing the woman to come out. The model should be placed out doors but not exposed to rain or sun.

The arches of the doorways may be made with a big bit ($1\frac{3}{8}''$) or a scroll saw. If a bit is used, bore a hole for the spur first, lest it split the board. While boring hold the board vertically in the vise. The portion cut off between the doorways can be sawed with the tip of the back-saw if the board is laid flat on the bench-hook. The slanting lines at the top, also, can be sawed while held down on the bench-hook. After the front, back and sides are made, nail the back to the sides, but screw the front. When this is done, put the house in the vise in an upright position and plane the tops of the sides slanting. Notice that one roof is wider than the other. Nail the narrower one first, with the grain running from front to back. Do not drive nails into the front but nail it securely at the back and side. Letting the plane rest on the other side of the house, plane the upper edge of this roof slanting, so that the other roof will fit. Nail this in place; set all nails; and plane the upper edge of this roof slanting, letting the plane rest on the first roof. Two brads may now be driven near the center of the ridge-pole to hold the roofs together. After making the floor, place the house in position on it ($\frac{1}{4}''$ from back, $\frac{1}{2}''$ from ends) and draw a line around the house. Remove the house; drive three brads straight down thru the floor; pull them out and start them from the under side in the same holes; then put the house in place again and drive the brads home. Put in more brads to hold the house securely.

To make the chimney, saw a notch $3/16''$ deep in the end of a $\frac{3}{4}''$ square stick. If it fits on the roof, bore a $5/16''$ hole thru its center, and saw the chimney off $\frac{3}{4}''$ long. Glue it $\frac{3}{8}''$ from the front end of the roof. When dry, bore the hole thru the roof.

The chimney top with the dowel attached to it below is made to revolve so that the Hygroscope may be adjusted. To make the chimney top, bore a $\frac{1}{4}''$ hole into the end of a $\frac{1}{2}''$ dowel; then saw it off $\frac{1}{2}''$ and glue in the upper dowel. Make the turntable somewhat round at each end. In the center of it, glue and nail the lower dowel. Next, paint the house if desired. The violin string is glued and wedged into holes in the upper and lower dowels so that the turntable will swing $3/16''$ above the floor.

The man and woman may be made of cardboard, wood, clay, chalk or plaster of Paris; or they can be bought at a toy store. Painted in bright colors and shellacked or varnished, they look well. They can be made to balance on the turntable by adding a piece of lead. Of course, neither they nor the turntable should touch any part of the house as they swing around.

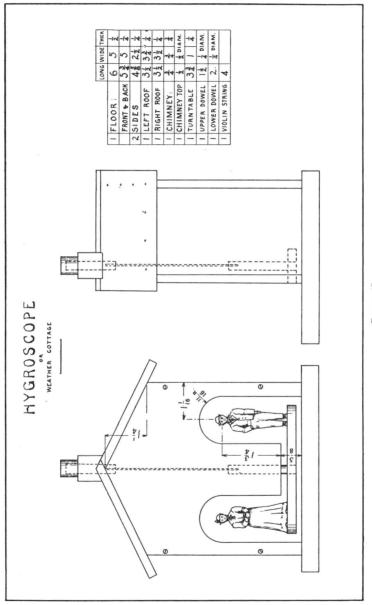

	LONG	WIDE	THICK
1 FLOOR	6	5	$\frac{1}{4}$
1 FRONT & BACK	$5\frac{3}{4}$	5	$\frac{1}{4}$
2 SIDES	$4\frac{3}{8}$	$2\frac{1}{2}$	$\frac{1}{4}$
1 LEFT ROOF	$3\frac{1}{2}$	$3\frac{1}{4}$	$\frac{1}{4}$
1 RIGHT ROOF	$3\frac{1}{2}$	$3\frac{1}{2}$	$\frac{1}{4}$
1 CHIMNEY	$\frac{3}{4}$	$\frac{3}{4}$	$\frac{3}{4}$
1 CHIMNEY TOP	$\frac{1}{4}$	$\frac{1}{2}$ DIAM.	
1 TURNTABLE	$3\frac{3}{4}$	1	$\frac{1}{4}$
1 UPPER DOWEL	$1\frac{1}{2}$	$\frac{1}{4}$ DIAM.	
1 LOWER DOWEL	2.	$\frac{1}{4}$ DIAM.	
1 VIOLIN STRING	4		

HYGROSCOPE

OR

WEATHER COTTAGE

PLATE 17

ELECTROPHORUS—Plate 18.

The electrophorus consists of two parts, a pan filled with a resinous mixture, and a cover which has been completely covered with tinfoil. Under favorable conditions, a spark of electricity ½″ long can be obtained from this electrophorus. The favorable conditions are these: The air should be dry; both parts of the electrophorus should be warm, dry, and clean; and the tinfoil and rosin should be perfectly flat, so as to come in close contact with each other.

Make the pan and its sides as shown in Plate 18. Glue and nail the sides in place and round their upper edges well with sandpaper. To make the resinous mixture, melt a half teacup of rosin with two teaspoons of turpentine and about the same of paraffin in a rather deep dish, and pour the mixture into the pan. As all these materials are inflammable, perhaps the safest place to melt them is in the oven. After the pan is cold, test the surface of the rosin to see that it is flat every way. If it is not flat, sandpaper the high parts slowly with coarse sandpaper.

When making the cover, observe the directions on page 20, then round the edge to a good half-circle. Test the cover also to see that it is flat, especially on its under side, for to get good sparks, the tinfoil and rosin must come just as close together as possible. Cut two circles of tinfoil 4½″ in diameter. Smooth them carefully on a piece of paper, spread glue thinly on the cover, lay the tinfoil on the glue, and smooth it with the fingers. Press the edges as smooth as possible because electricity escapes easily from sharp corners. Cover the larger open spaces with bits of tinfoil. Hard rubber (ebonite), being a non-conductor of electrity, makes the best handle. A piece of an old rubber comb or a fountain pen can be used for this purpose.

To get a spark of electricity, rub the rosin with soft leather, fur, or woolen; place the cover on it; touch the top of the cover with the finger (to remove the negative electricity); lift the cover by the top of the handle; bring the edge of the cover near a finger, or other conductor, and a spark will fly off with a snap. It is a miniature flash of lightning. Some books on electricity describe many other experiments which can be tried.

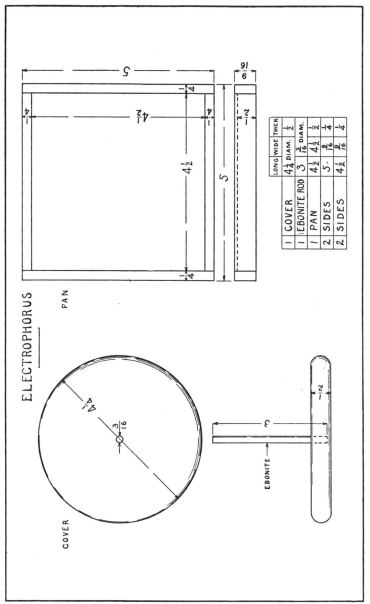

ELECTROPHORUS

PAN

COVER

EBONITE

		LONG	WIDE	THICK
1	COVER		$4\frac{1}{4}$ DIAM.	$\frac{1}{2}$
1	EBONITE ROD	3	$\frac{3}{16}$ DIAM.	
1	PAN	$4\frac{1}{2}$	$4\frac{1}{2}$	$\frac{1}{4}$
2	SIDES	5.	$\frac{9}{16}$	$\frac{1}{4}$
2	SIDES	$4\frac{1}{2}$	$\frac{9}{16}$	$\frac{1}{4}$

PLATE 18

WATERWHEEL—Plate 19.

This waterwheel is designed to be placed in a flowing stream. A longer trough might well lead the water into this one so as to get greater speed.

Make the trough first, being careful to make a good fit where the sides nail to the bottom. Nail the top 5″ from the end where the wheel is placed. The upper corners of the axle blocks are to be cut off 1″. The center of the 5/16″ hole for the axle is ⅞″ from the lower edge. When nailing the axle blocks in place, put a dowel or lead pencil thru the holes to help in nailing the blocks exactly opposite each other.

After sawing a board for the wheel 4¼″ square, draw the diagonals and diameters (cornerwise and crosswise, that means) to divide it into eight parts. Draw a 4″ circle for the wheel and a 3¼″ circle to mark the depth of the notches for the paddles. Shape the wheel. (See page 20 for directions.) Test it with the trysquare to keep the edge square with the flat surface. Bore a ¼″ hole in the center with the greatest care, or the wheel will wobble sidewise. The notches are cut with the back-saw alone. One-eighth of an inch to one side of the eight lines across the circle, saw straight down to the inner circle. Be careful to hold the saw square with the wheel. After this saw cut is made, measure the width of the notch by holding the edge of a paddle so as just to cover the saw cut, and, with a knife point make a dot at the other side of the paddle. Holding the trysquare against one side of the wheel and the inner edge of its blade over the dot, score a knife line across the edge of the wheel. Then saw straight down again *inside* this knife line. Saw cornerwise a few times and the wood will be removed sufficiently. The notches may better be too small than too large, for the paddles can be planed thinner to fit. Clean the wheel with the plane before nailing the paddles. All these paddles except one can be nailed with the wheel held in a corner of the vise. To nail that one, put a thin board upright in the vise and rest the wheel on its top. All nails should be started in the paddles, not in the wheel.

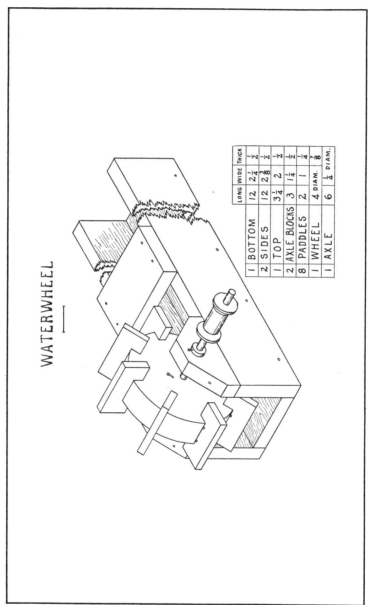

WATERWHEEL

		LONG	WIDE	THICK
1	BOTTOM	12	$2\frac{1}{4}$	$\frac{1}{2}$
2	SIDES	12	$2\frac{3}{8}$	$\frac{1}{2}$
1	TOP	$3\frac{1}{4}$	2	$\frac{1}{2}$
2	AXLE BLOCKS	3	$1\frac{1}{4}$	$\frac{1}{2}$
8	PADDLES	2	1	$\frac{1}{4}$
1	WHEEL	4 DIAM.		$\frac{7}{8}$
1	AXLE	6	$\frac{1}{4}$ DIAM.	

PLATE 19

Make the axle of hard wood. Push it thru the axle blocks and
wheel, and lock it to the wheel with a brad, Plate 19. The axle is
made long so that a pulley (spool) can be put on and a belt (string)
run from this to other pulleys. A leather washer outside each axle
block keeps the wheel in the center. If the work has been carefully
done, the paddles will not strike; if they do strike, they must be
pared off.

WATER MOTOR—PLATE 20.

This motor is a waterwheel designed for an ordinary hose faucet. Under a stream of water no bigger than a large needle, it will fairly buzz. If the wheel does not run exactly true on the axle, the motor will need legs screwed on the outside of the box.

Make the wheel of soft wood just as true as possible. (See page 20.) For the axle a small brass rod or a large knitting needle may be used. In the center of the wheel, drill a hole smaller than the axle so as to make a tight fit. Be very careful to bore this hole straight. Force the axle thru the wheel, and if the wheel wobbles only slightly drive wooden wedges beside the axle to force it square with the wheel. If it wobbles too much, plug the hole and try boring again. Resting the axle on the jaws of the vise, revolve the wheel rapidly to see where it is out of true, and patiently pare it down. The flat side of the wheel which wobbles only a little can be planed off. The strip of screen wire netting should now be tacked on the wheel. It is long enough to go twice around the wheel, and should be tacked on with a dozen small tacks.

For suggestions about the pulley see page 56.

Prepare a block of soft wood for the coupling. From its bottom, gage a line marking the height of the dovetails in which the blocks C and D fit $\frac{3}{8}''$ on each side. Saw these dovetails 3/16" deep, and pare them slanting with a chisel. In the center of the top, bore a 1" hole, $\frac{3}{4}''$ deep; continue the hole thru the block with a $\frac{1}{2}''$ bit. Bore holes $\frac{3}{8}''$ from the top, $\frac{1}{2}''$ from the ends for the two $1\frac{1}{2}''$ screws which are shown in the small drawing, Plate 20. Gage and saw out the left-hand half of the block (as shown in the plate) as deep as the 1" hole. The purpose of this is to permit a squeezing fit on the threads of the faucet. When first trying it on the faucet, squeeze it hard with a hand-screw to jamb the threads into the wood; after that, the screws can be put in and the coupling attached at pleasure. A $\frac{1}{4}''$ hole is bored in the $\frac{1}{2}''$ dowel, which serves as a nozzle, until the spur just shows. Without allowing the bit to bore any farther, turn it around enough so that the spur will wear the wood and thus make a tapering hole as shown in the sectional drawings.

Prepare the sides, ends, and top of the box, the three blocks, the key wedge, and the two stops. The wedge should be 1/16" wider at one end than the other and should fit the dovetail. Block C should fit the other. In the top piece, bore a ¾" hole in the middle 1¼" from the end. This hole is larger than the nozzle to allow for adjustments. All these parts must now be thoroly soaked with paraffin. Melt the paraffin, apply it with a brush to all surfaces, and drive it in with heat. During the process, the nozzle can be made fast in the coupling, using plenty of paraffin to make it water tight. See that the tiny outlet occupies the best position for directing the water onto the wheel. After the nozzle is cold again, the outlet should be carefully worked out again with the warm point of a big hat-pin or wire, filed to a good point.

Put the parts together as follows: Nail one side (the right in the plate) to the ends; screw the other side to ends; nail top to ends and first side only; nail block B to A; then A to the top. Unscrew the side and bore holes in the center of the sides for the axle. Make them fit nicely, then soak them with paraffin. Put the wheel, the side, the pulley, and the stops in place. Put the coupling in such position that the nozzle comes over the rim of the wheel and nail block C. After putting two or three soft leather washers in the coupling screw it to the faucet, lock it to the motor, and the motor is ready.

Better bearings for the axle can be made of two pieces of solder screwed to the inside of the sides. If these are made, the holes in the sides should be large enough not to touch the axle. The wheel and pulley can be locked to a brass axle by boring a hole thru the axle with a drill made of a needle. (See Drills, page 11.)

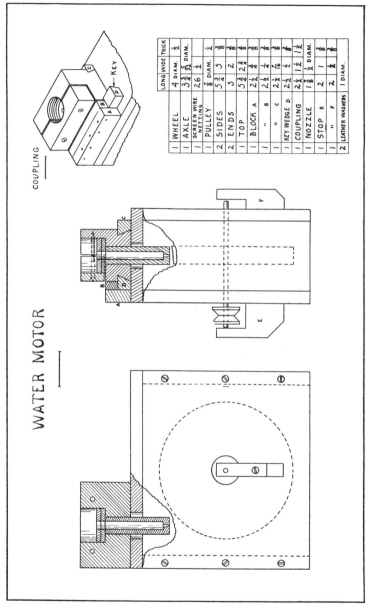

WATER MOTOR

COUPLING

KEY

	LONG	WIDE	THICK
1 WHEEL	4 DIAM.		$\frac{1}{2}$
1 AXLE	$3\frac{3}{4}$	$\frac{5}{32}$ DIAM.	
1 SCREEN WIRE NETTING	26	$\frac{1}{2}$	$\frac{1}{2}$
1 PULLEY	$\frac{7}{8}$ DIAM.		$\frac{1}{2}$
2 SIDES	$5\frac{3}{4}$	5	$\frac{3}{8}$
2 ENDS	5	2	$\frac{3}{8}$
1 TOP	$5\frac{3}{4}$	$2\frac{3}{4}$	$\frac{3}{8}$
1 BLOCK A	$2\frac{1}{2}$	$\frac{3}{4}$	$\frac{3}{8}$
1 " B	$2\frac{1}{2}$	$\frac{1}{4}$	$\frac{3}{8}$
1 " C	$2\frac{1}{2}$	$\frac{7}{16}$	$\frac{3}{8}$
1 KEY WEDGE D	$2\frac{1}{2}$	$\frac{1}{2}$	$\frac{3}{8}$
1 COUPLING	$2\frac{1}{2}$	$1\frac{1}{2}$	
1 NOZZLE	$1\frac{7}{8}$	$\frac{1}{2}$ DIAM.	
1 STOP E	2	1	$\frac{3}{8}$
1 " F	2	$\frac{1}{2}$	$\frac{3}{8}$
2 LEATHER WASHERS	1 DIAM.		

PLATE 20

SAND WHEEL—Plate 21.

Fine sand will make a wheel like this spin around lively. Most of the parts are easily made, the wheel offering the most difficulties.

As shown in the drawing it consists of two boxes, uprights connecting the two, and a wheel with paddles swung on an axle between the uprights.

To make the curves on the uprights, lay them edge to edge in the vise and start the spur of a large bit in the crack, 1½″ from each end. If a big spool cannot be obtained for the wheel, plane out an octagonal block 1⅜″ long, 1″ in diameter. The slanting part of the spool must be whittled away. Divide one end into eight equal parts and drawn lines lengthwise the spool at each division. On

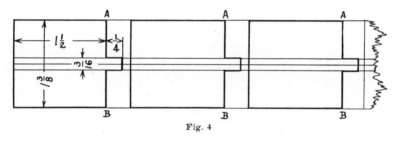

Fig. 4

these lines, measure very carefully 11/16″ from one end. Then, holding the spool level in the vise bore 3/16″ holes half thru the spool at each of these dots. The easiest way to lay out the paddles is in one long piece as shown in Fig. 4. If lines A and B are sawed carefully (see page 12) they will fit the spool well enough to glue. The stems of the paddles go into the holes bored in the spool. They are easily made round by paring the corners a little, and then screwing them around in a 3/16″ hole in a piece of hard wood. The ends of the paddles where the sand strikes are bevelled on the under side. The holes in the uprights, thru which 1¼″ brads are pushed into the center of the spool, must be exactly opposite each other, 3¼″ from the bottom. Little leather washers should be

SAND WHEEL

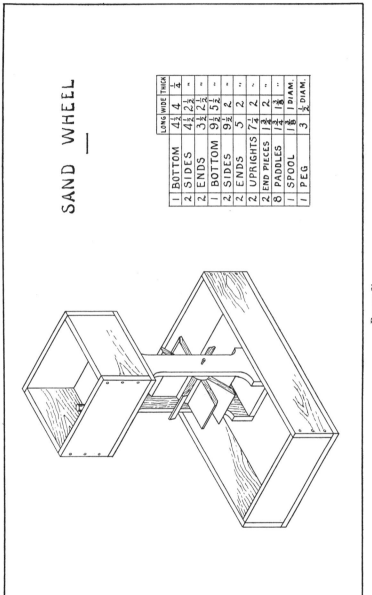

	LONG	WIDE	THICK
1 BOTTOM	4½	4	¼
2 SIDES	4½	2½	"
2 ENDS	3½	2½	"
1 BOTTOM	9½	5½	"
2 SIDES	9½	2	"
2 ENDS	5	2	"
2 UPRIGHTS	7¼	2	"
2 END PIECES	1¾	2	"
8 PADDLES	1¾	1⅜	"
1 SPOOL	1⅜	1 DIAM.	
1 PEG	3	½ DIAM.	

PLATE 21

put between the spool and the uprights. Now make the boxes. To nail the boxes to the upright follow the suggestions on page 59 for nailing the floor of the weather cottage. Keep the brads near the center of the uprights lest they split the curves. A 5/16″ hole for the sand is bored in the upper box in such a position that the sand will strike near the middle of the ends of the paddles. The peg is tapered to fit this hole.

RUNNING WHEEL—Plate 22.

It is fine fun for several boys to race down the street with running wheels. Each boy can have a different kind of wheel by following the suggestions on Plate 22.

The wheel may be made any convenient size. Saw a board off square and plane it flat. To be sure that it is flat, it must be tested with a straight-edge from corner to corner, crosswise, and lengthwise. Draw the circle with a string pinned to the center, if a large com-

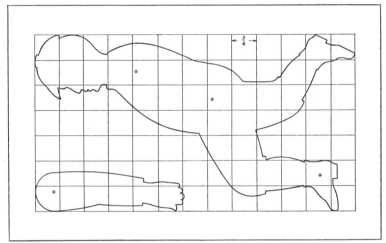

Fig. 5

pass is not at hand. Saw it with a turning saw and finish it as suggested on page 20. Bore and countersink a hole in the center for a 1½″ flat-head screw. Make the handle and drill a small hole in it where the wheel is to be screwed on. Round off the upper end and edges of the handle so that it feels good to the hand grasping it. The screws used in the connecting rod should slip easily thru the holes at each end. Altho one arm will do, two look better. To draw the boy, draw as many ¾″ squares on the board as there are in Fig. 5, then sketch the outline one square at a time. To cut it out, a scroll-saw or turning-saw is almost surely needed, tho a patient boy can do it with auger-bits, back-saw, knife, and file—the bits to be used first at all the inside angles. On the handle, must be put a block on which to screw the boy. To fasten the two arms loosely at the shoulders, the screw should be loose in the shoulder and first arm, and tight in the second arm. The same is true of the hands and flagpole. In the top of the flagpole, bore a hole to fit a small flag. Paint of bright colors makes the model look much more pleasing.

An easy way to make the sliding part of the lower right-hand running wheel, Plate 22, is to cut out with bit and chisel a narrow slot thru the handle, wide enough for two screws, with washers on them, which screw into the block holding the flag.

READY FOR A RACE

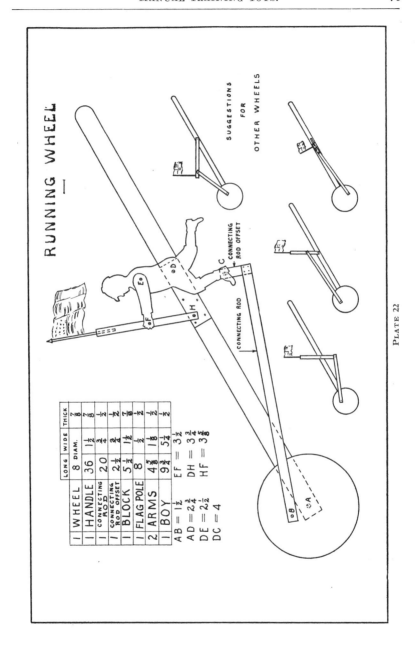

RUNNING WHEEL

SUGGESTIONS FOR OTHER WHEELS

CONNECTING ROD OFFSET

CONNECTING ROD

		LONG	WIDE	THICK
1	WHEEL	8 DIAM.		$\frac{7}{8}$
1	HANDLE	36	$1\frac{1}{2}$	$\frac{7}{8}$
1	CONNECTING ROD	20	$\frac{3}{4}$	$\frac{1}{2}$
1	CONNECTING ROD OFFSET	$2\frac{1}{2}$	$\frac{3}{4}$	$\frac{1}{2}$
1	BLOCK	$5\frac{1}{2}$	$1\frac{1}{2}$	$\frac{7}{8}$
1	FLAG POLE	8	$\frac{1}{2}$	$\frac{1}{2}$
2	ARMS	$4\frac{5}{8}$	$1\frac{8}{8}$	$\frac{1}{2}$
1	BOY	$9\frac{3}{4}$	$5\frac{1}{4}$	$\frac{1}{2}$

AB = $1\frac{3}{4}$ EF = $3\frac{1}{2}$
AD = $2\frac{3}{4}$ DH = $3\frac{3}{4}$
DE = $2\frac{1}{2}$ HF = $3\frac{5}{8}$
DC = 4

PLATE 22

RATTLE—Plate 23.

This is a noisy toy and will make a safe substitute for fire-crackers on the Fourth of July. Some of the dimensions may be changed to suit such a spool as can be obtained. It should be a rather deep spool, that is, one that held a lot of thread.

The noise is made by the spring snapping off the slats in the spool as the head of the rattle is swung round and round. Draw lines across one end of the spool to divide it into eight equal parts. Place the spool endwise in the vise and, with the back-saw, cut eight notches a little more than 1/16" wide straight towards the opposite side of the spool. By sawing twice at each notch, the wood which remains can easily be removed with the saw held slanting. There are several ways of making the eight little slats which fit into these notches; the easiest, perhaps, is to split them from a block (1⅝"x1½"x-5/16") of a straight-grained wood, and plane them on the jig described at the foot of page 19. Glue them in the notches. Plane the back and the spring this same way. Square both ends of the back but do not plane it quite to width until it is glued and nailed in place. In the two sides, bore a 5/16" hole for the dowel, ¾" from the end and a little over ¾" from the back edge. (Holes are always located by their centers.) This dowel must fit tightly in the handle and spool, and loosely in the two sides. Plane the spring thinner at the narrow end. It should be narrow enough and its corners cut off enough so as not to touch the spool when it snaps. The handle might well be octagonal rather than round.

The parts may now be put together as follows: Glue and nail the sides first to the thick end, second to the thin end. The distance between the ends inside is 3 5/16". Keep these four parts flush on the back edges so that the back will fit. Glue and nail the back. Glue the dowel in the handle. Put glue inside the spool and on the middle portion of the dowel, then, with the spool between the two sides, push the dowel thru all three holes. Glue and nail the spring in place. It should be as far towards the spool as it will go without snapping the next slat when it snaps off one slat.

RATTLE

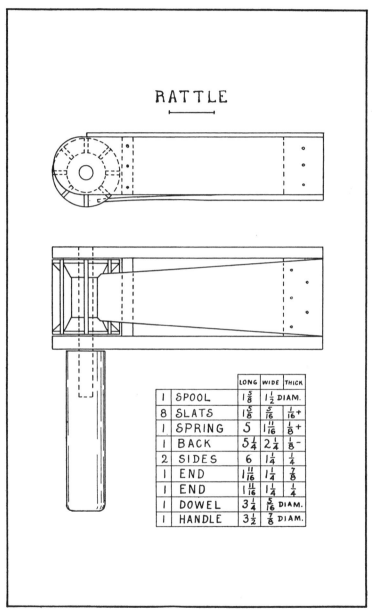

		LONG	WIDE	THICK
1	SPOOL	$1\frac{5}{8}$	$1\frac{1}{2}$ DIAM.	
8	SLATS	$1\frac{5}{8}$	$\frac{5}{16}$	$\frac{1}{16}+$
1	SPRING	5	$1\frac{11}{16}$	$\frac{1}{8}+$
1	BACK	$5\frac{1}{4}$	$2\frac{1}{4}$	$\frac{1}{8}-$
2	SIDES	6	$1\frac{1}{4}$	$\frac{1}{4}$
1	END	$1\frac{11}{16}$	$1\frac{1}{4}$	$\frac{7}{8}$
1	END	$1\frac{11}{16}$	$1\frac{1}{4}$	$\frac{1}{4}$
1	DOWEL	$3\frac{1}{4}$	$\frac{5}{16}$ DIAM.	
1	HANDLE	$3\frac{1}{2}$	$\frac{7}{8}$ DIAM.	

PLATE 23

CART—PLATE 24.

The important features of a cart are the wheels and axle and the tongue; if these are strong and the tongue securely fastened, almost any box will do for the body. Two tongues, nailed or screwed to the sides of the body, probably make the strongest handle, but they are not so good looking as the one shown in Plate 24. If this one is screwed to the box with six 1″ screws, two in the tongue and two in each block, it will be strong enough. Some of the nicer boxes to be secured of a grocer will do for a body, tho it is better to make one one's self.

Four wheels of ½″ hard wood should be made (see page 20) and then each two of the four glued and nailed together very securely with the grain crosswise. For this purpose, 1¼″ clout, or clinch nails are best. Do not drive them too near the center nor the rim. To clinch nails, they should be driven onto a piece of iron. After this is done, a ⅞″ hole (or larger if you can get a larger stick for the axle) is bored straight thru the center. To cut the cylindrical ends of the axle, first draw a ⅞″ circle at the center of each end, then lay out and saw out two rectangular pieces, one on each side of the circles so as to leave a ⅞″ square pin, 2¼″ long. Proceed to make these pins; first, eight sided; then, sixteen sided; then, round; using knife or chisel and a coarse flat file. Make the hole in the washers before cutting off each corner 9/16″. These washers are to be fastened to the axle when held rather snugly against the wheel with two 1″ screws put crosswise the grain. Before putting the wheels on the last time, rub the axles and holes well with hard soap to make them run easier. Draw a line across the bottom of the body 5″ from the back end, and bore four screw holes thru the bottom; countersink them well on the inside of the body, and put 1″ screws thru into the flat side of the axle. The axle is planned so that the wheels run within ⅛″ of the body.

With a curved lower edge, the tongue is 2½″ wide at one end and 1½″ at the other. To get the correct slant at the wide end, block up the cart level, have some one (or the vise) hold the tongue in the position wanted when finished, then with a strip of wood

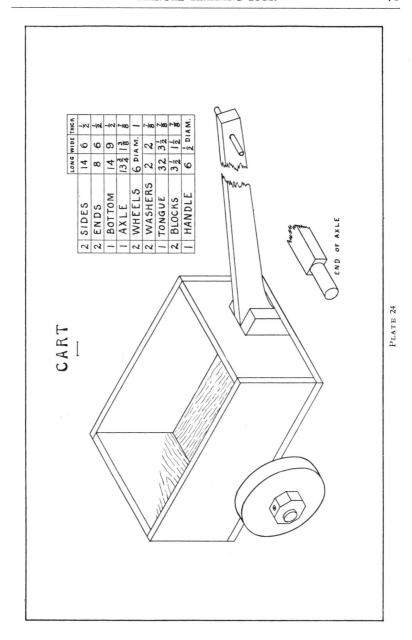

CART

	LONG	WIDE	THICK
2 SIDES	14	6	$\frac{1}{2}$
2 ENDS	8	6	$\frac{1}{2}$
1 BOTTOM	14	9	$\frac{1}{2}$
1 AXLE	$13\frac{3}{4}$	$1\frac{3}{8}$	$\frac{7}{8}$
2 WHEELS	6 DIAM.		1
2 WASHERS	2	2	$\frac{7}{8}$
1 TONGUE	32	$3\frac{1}{2}$	$\frac{7}{8}$
2 BLOCKS	$3\frac{1}{2}$	$1\frac{1}{2}$	$\frac{7}{8}$
1 HANDLE	6	$\frac{1}{2}$ DIAM.	

END OF AXLE

PLATE 24

— 6

about 2″ wide placed upright against the front of the body, draw a line on the tongue. From the lowest corner of the tongue, draw another line parallel to the first, and saw off. After making the two blocks and fastening them securely to the tongue, saw the lower ends flush with the curve of the tongue. Place the tongue in position, draw a line around it on the body, then bore holes where screws will go best into the tongue and blocks. Six 1″ screws well countersunk will hold the tongue securely. Since the tongue is fastened to the *front,* the sides and bottom must be well nailed to *it;* or, the corners may be strengthened with a piece of tin inside and outside each corner, tacked or riveted together. Each piece of tin should be about 3″ square.

A piece of old bicycle frame forced tightly into the hole of a wheel, makes it very durable. Such a hole would doubtless have to be bored with an expansive bit. A bicycle frame is easily filed in two at some distance from the reinforced joints. Such a piece should be longer than the thickness of the wheel to allow filing it flush after it is driven in. To force it in, use a strong vise, or, after protecting it with hard wood, drive it slowly with a heavy hammer.

Small carts can be made with wheels made of spools like those of the cannon. (See Plate 25.)

CANNON—PLATE 25.

This cannon will shoot small marbles very well. The force of it depends, of course, on the strength of the rubber bands. Because the ramrod and handle are rather heavy, a strong dowel is put thru the handle and ramrod. The rubber washer absorbs some of the shock.

For the barrel draw a $1\frac{1}{4}''$ circle on one end of a stick $6\frac{1}{2}''$x $1\frac{1}{2}''$x$1\frac{1}{2}''$. From the center of this circle, bore a 9/16" hole straight thru the stick endwise, stopping as soon as the spur comes thru. Set the needle of the compass in this spur hole and draw a 1" circle and, if possible, a $1\frac{1}{4}''$ circle; then finish boring.

Plane the stick round to the $1\frac{1}{4}''$ circle. To hold the stick while doing this, put a rod thru the hole, open the vise $6\frac{1}{2}''$ and let the barrel rest endwise in the vise. Two and one-half inches from the breech end of the barrel, draw a line around it to limit the taper of the muzzle end. Plane the muzzle to the 1" circle. Two inches from the breech, bore a $\frac{3}{8}''$ hole straight thru the barrel; and into this hole glue the axle. After the glue is dry, bore out the barrel again, and sandpaper the hole well.

Make the ramrod fit loosely in the barrel. (See directions for Dart, page 16.) Make the handle in the same manner as the barrel was made, except that, after drawing the $1\frac{1}{4}''$ circle at the end where the spur just appears, the hole is *not* bored further. Glue the ramrod in place, and fasten it with the $\frac{3}{8}''$ dowel. The curved notch into which the rubber bands are tied, can be worked out patiently with a round file, first cutting a V-shaped notch with a knife. Pare the corners and sandpaper all parts well.

The rubber washer can be made of an old rubber heel. To bore a hole in it, squeeze it between two boards and bore thru both together.

At least one of the uprights must be screwed to the base. The first one may be nailed. Glue and nail this one $\frac{1}{4}''$ from the edge of the base. Hold the other in place and draw a line around it. Bore holes for the screws, put the screws in the holes, and press the upright on them to mark where to bore in the upright. After boring in the uprights, put the cannon and upright in place, and tighten the screws. The wheels can be made of the ends of large spools, well counter-sunk for a short, large screw.

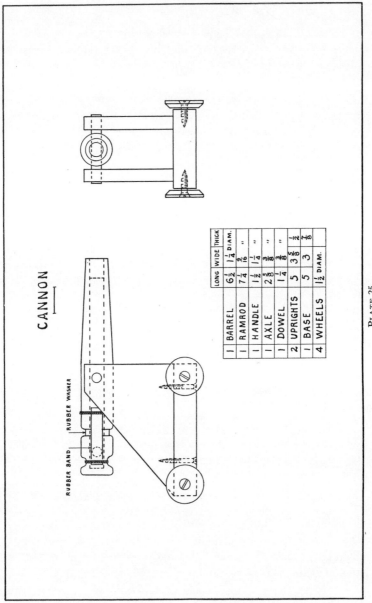

CANNON

		LONG	WIDE	THICK
1	BARREL	$6\frac{1}{2}$	$1\frac{1}{4}$ DIAM.	
1	RAMROD	$7\frac{1}{4}$	$\frac{9}{16}$	"
1	HANDLE	$1\frac{1}{2}$	$\frac{1}{4}$	"
1	AXLE	$2\frac{5}{8}$	$\frac{3}{8}$	"
1	DOWEL	$1\frac{1}{4}$	$\frac{3}{8}$	"
2	UPRIGHTS	5	$3\frac{5}{8}$	$\frac{1}{2}$
1	BASE	5	3	$\frac{7}{8}$
4	WHEELS	$1\frac{1}{2}$ DIAM.		

RUBBER BAND   RUBBER WASHER

PLATE 25

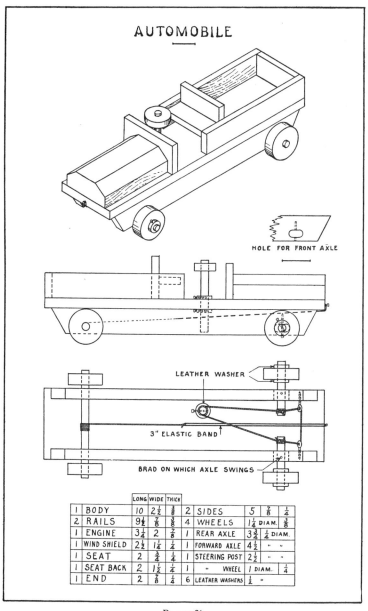

AUTOMOBILE

HOLE FOR FRONT AXLE

LEATHER WASHER

3" ELASTIC BAND

BRAD ON WHICH AXLE SWINGS

		LONG	WIDE	THICK					
I	BODY	10	$2\frac{1}{2}$	$\frac{3}{8}$	2	SIDES	5	$\frac{7}{8}$	$\frac{1}{4}$
2	RAILS	$9\frac{1}{2}$	$\frac{7}{8}$	$\frac{3}{8}$	4	WHEELS	$1\frac{1}{4}$ DIAM.		$\frac{3}{8}$
I	ENGINE	$3\frac{1}{4}$	2	$\frac{7}{8}$	I	REAR AXLE	$3\frac{3}{4}$	$\frac{1}{4}$ DIAM.	
I	WIND SHIELD	$2\frac{1}{2}$	$1\frac{1}{4}$	$\frac{1}{4}$	I	FORWARD AXLE	$4\frac{1}{2}$	"	"
I	SEAT	2	$\frac{3}{4}$	$\frac{1}{4}$	I	STEERING POST	$2\frac{1}{2}$	"	"
I	SEAT BACK	2	$1\frac{1}{2}$	$\frac{1}{4}$	I	" WHEEL	I DIAM.		$\frac{1}{4}$
I	END	2	$\frac{7}{8}$	$\frac{1}{4}$	6	LEATHER WASHERS	$\frac{1}{2}$ "		

PLATE 26

AUTOMOBILE—PLATE 26.

Tho the motor (an elastic band) which makes this automobile go is a short-winded affair, still, if the wheels are easy running, it will go alone for a short distance on a wooden floor. A stronger elastic can be used if the automobile carries a load. If the parts are painted with bright colors before they are entirely put together, the automobile will look very well.

First, make the body, then 4¼″ from the front end and ¾″ from the right side, bore a 1/4″ hole in the body for the steering post. This should fit tightly so as to hold the wheels in any position desired. Leather washers are nailed to the post close to the body. The steering post must be put in place before any other parts are fastened to the body.

The ends of the rails which are later fastened to the bottom of the body, slant ½″. The center of the holes for the axles is ¾″ beyond this slanting line and ¼″ above the lower edge of the rails. When boring these ¼″ holes, the rails should be clamped together so that the holes will be exactly opposite each other. The forward holes are made long to allow the axles to swing back and forth. To make this hole, two ¼″ holes are bored side by side and the top and bottom smoothed with a ¼″ chisel. When nailing the body to the rails, put the rear axle thru the holes to aid in keeping them opposite each other.

The forward axle is made in one piece and kept so until after the steering "rope" is in place. The axle must be held carefully in place while the brad holes are bored ⅛″ from the outer edge of the rails and straight thru the center of the axle. A tight fitting brad is driven into this hole. The steering rope must not stretch; large, hard thread is suitable. Wind a piece about 18″ long tightly around the axle about ¼″ from one rail and tie it. Pass one end thru the small screw-eyes shown in the lower drawing, and wind it around the axle near the other rail leaving no slack in the screw-eyes; then wind six to eight turns smoothly around the steering post, and fasten the end to the beginning with several half-hitches. (See Plate 15.) A separate thread should be tied around the axle and steering rope at the second place. Should there be any slack, it can be taken up by laying a V-shaped thread over the steering rope near the axle and passing the two ends over the upper side of the axle, and tying them across the steering rope on the other side of the axle. This tends to pull the steering rope together on top of the axle.

The wheels can be sawed from short lengths of curtain poles, obtained at a furniture store. The $\frac{1}{4}''$ holes for the axle, must be bored exactly at the center. The wheels must turn freely on the front axle, but be glued to the rear axle, which must itself turn freely in the rails. After the wheels are in place, the front axle can be sawed in two with a back-saw, using very short strokes, and sawing two cuts nearly thru before either is sawed completely.

Nail the wind-shield to the engine, then glue both to the body. Nail the seat-back to the seat so that the top of the seat will be $\frac{3}{4}''$ above the body, then nail the two sides to the end and to the seat-back and seat. Glue the whole to the body. Nails can be driven up thru the body into the engine, the seat back, and the end, if care is used in locating them.

One end of the elastic band (motor) is tied with a bit of string to a brad driven in the forward end of the body of the automobile. On the other end of the elastic band is tied a piece of string about $8''$ long. This is put just under the body and above the steering rope and wound two or three times tightly around the rear axle and tied. The string and elastic band should be simply straight, the elastic neither stretched nor loose. To wind up the motor, move the automobile backwards on the floor and hold the rear wheels until ready to let the automobile go.

BOW PISTOL—PLATE 27.

For target shooting in the house, this is a fine toy. With nicely made arrows and a good bow, it will shoot very well.

Make a good bow of rattan, or other tough wood. An old spoke of a carriage wheel could doubtless be obtained of a blacksmith or wheelwright, and such a hickory spoke would make a good bow.

Make the bow much like that shown on Plate 8, except that it should be round at the center to fit the ⅜" hole in the pistol. The bow-string should be a hard cord so that it will slip easily from the notches in the barrel when the trigger is pulled.

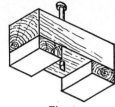

Fig. 6

Before shaping the pistol, make the groove in the center of one edge of the board. This should be made with a ⅜" round plane. It can be made, however, with the tool shown in Fig. 6, a gouge, and a round file. This tool is much like the one described on page 41 tho a larger nail is used. Make the groove 7/32" deep; gage a line 3/16" from each side of the board; then use the gouge inside these lines and as deep as the groove. When the gouging is well done, smooth the groove with a round file or coarse sandpaper wrapped around a pencil.

Draw and shape the pistol. Make the lower edge of the barrel half round. Sandpaper it well. Make the trigger of hard wood and screw it on the pistol. The shape of the notch next to the trigger is very important but the shape of the other one is not so. Both notches, however, must be so smooth and well rounded as not to injure the bowstring. They should be not deeper than one-half the depth of the groove.

Arrows are quickly made by sawing long strips of straight-grained wood, 3/16" square, planing the corners, and sandpapering; then cutting them 5" long, splitting the ends (see page 16), inserting a paper 1"x½" and tying the end with thread.

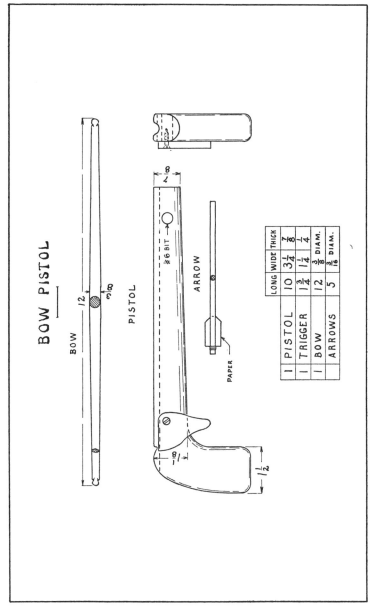

BOW PISTOL

BOW

12

PISTOL

8

#6 BIT

ARROW

PAPER

1/2

8/1

		LONG	WIDE	THICK
1	PISTOL	10	$3\frac{1}{4}$	$\frac{7}{8}$
1	TRIGGER	$1\frac{3}{4}$	$1\frac{1}{4}$	$\frac{1}{4}$
1	BOW	12	$\frac{3}{8}$ DIAM.	
	ARROWS	5	$\frac{3}{16}$ DIAM.	

PLATE 27

ELASTIC GUN—Plate 28.

If cash carrier elastic cord about 5/16″ in diameter and 18″ long is used on this gun, it will shoot buckshot, peas, small arrows, etc., with considerable force; in fact, if the cord is fastened far enough forward, it will require all a boy's strength to pull the rider back to the hook. The gun may be made of pine, whitewood or clear spruce.

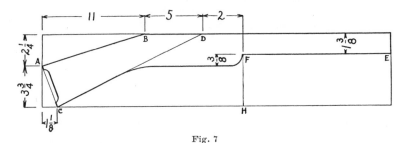

Fig. 7

To lay out the gun (see Fig. 7) first draw A B, then A C, then measure B D and draw C D; next measure the width of the barrel and draw E F; add ⅜″ below this for the gun-stock, and finally draw the curves freehand. To saw it out, first rip it along E F, then cross cut it at H F, then rip it as far the curve along C D, and then along the lower side of the gun-stock to meet C D, finally along A B. Of course, none of this sawing should quite touch the lines. Plane to these lines wherever possible, then use the spokeshave. The curve and corner at F should be pared with a chisel. The lower edge of the gun-stock and barrel is made half-round, but the upper edge, especially where the spring is screwed, is only slightly round. The curve at the butt of the gun-stock should be cut out with the turning-saw, and rounded with a half-round file. The groove can be made as in the bow pistol. (See page 86.)

All parts of the gun should be well sandpapered, especially where the elastic will rub on the barrel.

Make the trigger of tough wood.

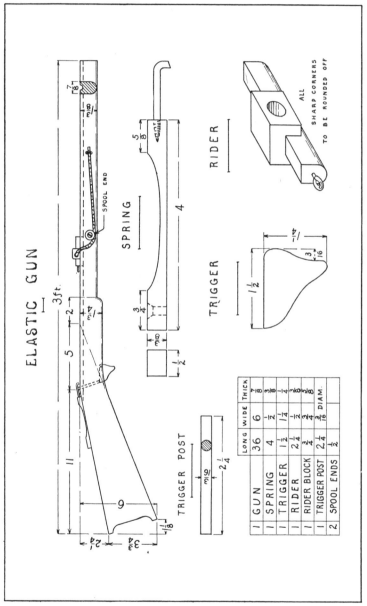

ELASTIC GUN

3 ft.

SPOOL END

SPRING

RIDER

ALL SHARP CORNERS TO BE ROUNDED OFF

TRIGGER

TRIGGER POST

	LONG	WIDE	THICK
1 GUN	36	6	$\frac{7}{8}$
1 SPRING	4	$\frac{1}{2}$	$\frac{3}{8}$
1 TRIGGER	$1\frac{1}{2}$	$1\frac{1}{4}$	$\frac{1}{4}$
1 RIDER	$2\frac{1}{4}$	$\frac{1}{2}$	$\frac{3}{8}$
1 RIDER BLOCK	$\frac{3}{4}$	$\frac{3}{4}$	$\frac{5}{8}$
1 TRIGGER POST	$2\frac{1}{4}$	$\frac{9}{16}$ DIAM.	
2 SPOOL ENDS	$\frac{1}{2}$		

PLATE 28

Bore a $\frac{1}{4}''$ hole for the trigger post about $\frac{3}{4}''$ from the back end of the groove, making it slant forward about $\frac{3}{4}''$. Make this hole smooth as possible. Where the hole comes thru the gun-stock, start the mortise in which the trigger belongs. This should be $\frac{3}{8}''$ deep and an easy fit for the trigger. Put the trigger in place, and drill a small hole straight thru the gun-stock and trigger. Consider carefully where to bore this hole so that it will not come too near the edge of the trigger. Insert a good-fitting brad and see if the trigger post will move up and down about $\frac{1}{4}''$. Do not make the mortise so long that the trigger post will slip by the trigger.

Now make the spring of hard wood. Pare the curve from each end with a chisel, holding the spring endwise in the bench-hook. The holes for the screw and the hook must be large enough so that the spring will not be split, and yet the hook must be screwed in strongly to hold the elastic. The hook must be filed off enough, and slanting, so that the screw-eye in the rider will slide under it and be caught.

The rider is the hardest part to make because it is small and must be of hard wood; also, the block must be nicely fitted into the long piece. Make the lower edge of the long piece round so as to slide well in the groove. Bore a $5/16''$ hole thru the block *endwise* the grain, countersink the ends, and smooth them so that they cannot injure the elastic. Next lay out, saw, and chisel a notch $5/16''$ deep in the long piece in which the block will fit snugly. Glue it and nail it from the under side, or put in a $\frac{1}{2}''$ screw. Holes will have to be bored carefully for either brads or screw. Bore a hole, and put the screw-eye in such a position that it will slide under the hook with a snap. Be careful not to twist the eye off in this hard wood. The back end of the eye might well be filed somewhat slanting so as to slip under the hook better.

Put the elastic thru the rider, snap the rider on the hook, and pull the ends of the elastic as far as seems best,—don't have it too strong! Where the ends of the elastic are pulled, bore two $\frac{1}{4}''$ holes thru the barrel one above the other. Bind the elastic securely between these holes; to make it doubly secure, wind a string between the elastic and the barrel to pull the first strings closer together.

Now saw off the ends of a spool about ½" and screw them to the barrel in such a place that they will hold the elastic, without stretching, against the sides of the barrel. These spools should turn easily. They cannot be placed exactly opposite because the screws will interfere.

Snap the rider to the hook, pull the trigger, and notice that the rider goes up with the trigger post. To hold it down, put a slender ¾" screw on each side of the groove in such a place that the screw heads will come over the outside of the screw-eye; or, 1" brads may be bent over the screw-eye. When everything is in working order, drive a 1" brad on each side of the spring to keep the hook always in place.

THE ELASTIC GUN

RATTLE-BANG GUN—Plate 29.

For boys who want to play soldier, here is a gun which will make a big noise but will not hurt anybody.

First, make the rattle of maple. The slot in it can be made with the rip-saw. The solid end must be nicely squared to fit the forward end of the pocket cut out of the gun-stock. Here it must be held firmly in place by glue and two screws. One screw is put slanting from the top of the gun-stock; the other is put straight from the bottom. That the rattle may sound the loudest, it must not touch anywhere else than this solid end. When putting the knocker and trigger in place, see that they also do not touch the rattle. The gun-stock is made like that of the elastic gun (Plate 28) except that it has to be 2⅜″ wide in that portion which holds the rattle. The pocket is 3½″ from the forward end and 1½″ deep where the solid part of the rattle fits. To put the slanting screw in nicely, a place must be cut out with a small chisel for its head, ⅜″ deep and ½″ away from the pocket. Clamp the rattle in position, bore a hole for the screw, then glue and screw the rattle in place. Before the glue is dry, see that the rattle is straight, then put the lower screw into it.

Make the knocker of maple. The reason for the triangular notch in its bottom edge will be evident when the trigger is turned around. The stiffer the spring is, the harder, of course, it will strike the rattle, and also, the harder the trigger will turn; ⅛″ will be thick enough for the thinnest place.

The trigger should also be of maple. Join it with a cross-lap joint. (See page 24.) Then, holding each end successively upright in the vise, draw the slanting lines and saw for ⅜″ lengthwise in such a way as to leave 1/16″ flat on each of the two adjacent surfaces. After sawing endwise, saw the little corner pieces off crosswise. The trigger has to withstand considerable pulling, so it should fit nicely, yet easily, a 1″ screw in its center. Before screwing either the knocker or the trigger in place, lay both on the gun-stock so that they will engage properly; then mark the place for the screws, drill holes, and screw them on. If the knocker touches

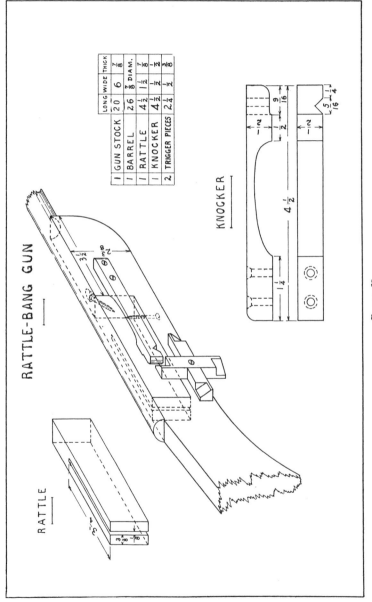

RATTLE-BANG GUN

RATTLE

KNOCKER

	LONG	WIDE	THICK
1 GUN STOCK	20	6	$\frac{7}{8}$
1 BARREL	26	$\frac{7}{8}$ DIAM.	$\frac{7}{8}$
1 RATTLE	$4\frac{1}{2}$	$1\frac{1}{2}$	$\frac{1}{2}$
1 KNOCKER	$4\frac{1}{2}$	$1\frac{1}{2}$	$\frac{1}{2}$
2 TRIGGER PIECES	$2\frac{1}{4}$	$1\frac{1}{2}$	$\frac{3}{8}$

PLATE 29

the rattle, take it off and plane a slanting chip or two where it is screwed to the gun-stock. A thin leather washer ⅝″ in diameter will prevent the trigger touching. A little soap will make the trigger turn easier.

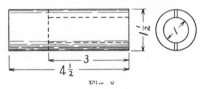

Fig. 8

   The barrel may well be made of a broomstick. To make it fit on the top of the gun-stock, saw it down the middle and cut off the lower half. Before fastening it in place, be sure that it will not touch the sounding part of the rattle.

   A still louder and more difficult rattle to make is shown in Fig. 8. Most boys would find it impossible to a bore a 1″ hole endwise in maple. The knocker and trigger would both have to be set out from the gun-stock.

BOAT—PLATE 30.

This boat is designed rather heavy to insure good service. It has ballast and beam enough to right itself even tho the sails do get wet. If a better looking boat is desired, draw the deck more slender; hollow the hull with bit and gouge; pare the gunwales with the spokeshave to give it some sheer; and nail on a thin deck. Soft pine is the best wood for the hull and spruce for the spars.

To lay out the hull, draw a center-line lengthwise on top, bottom, and ends of the block of wood. Make all the measurements given on the deck; (top of the hull, Plate 30) first lengthwise, then crosswise. Square with the deck, the curve should be worked out with rip-saw and spokeshave. The stem should next be undercut with the saws (rip and crosscut) so as to make place for the rudder. On the bottom leave a flat place $7\frac{1}{4}"x\frac{1}{2}"$ for the keel to fit; then round the hull as suggested by the sectional drawings at AB and CD.

Make the keel and nail it securely in place. From the under side of the boat and slanting the same as the keel and under-cut, bore a $\frac{5}{8}"$ hole for the stem of the rudder.

Make the rudder and tiller of $\frac{1}{4}"$ wood. The little mortise in the tiller can be cut with a small chisel after a $3/16"$ hole is bored at its center. For the wheel, make a dowel about $2"$ long and into one end of it bore a hole about $1"$ deep for a $1\frac{1}{4}"$ screw. Saw a piece from this end $\frac{5}{8}"$ long and screw it to the deck about $1\frac{1}{2}"$ in front of the hole bored for the rudder. The wheel should turn rather hard so as to stay in any position desired.

To make the spars, (mast, boom, etc.,) follow the directions on page 16. Use large screw-eyes in the gaff and boom (or see Plate 16, "method of swinging booms to mast") and a very small one at the top of the mast. To nail the bowsprit securely, place it $1"$ back of the prow, drive a $1"$ brad thru it near the prow, and one on each side of it $\frac{3}{4}"$ back. Bend these latter over the bowsprit before they are driven in their full length. An upward slant is given to the bowsprit by planing its larger end slanting to fit the deck.

7—

The rudder is hung on two staples made of pins. Two headless pins are driven into the rudder and bent down at right angles to slip into these staples. In order that the stem of the rudder may turn enough, the rudder must be hung close to the hull. Each "rope" of the rigging should have its own screw-eye (or staple) and cleat on the deck. The cleat (a device for fastening a "rope" in any position, by winding it back and forth) is simply two slender brads driven slanting.

The mainsail should be 9" on the mast and 11" at its outer edge. It should be hemmed and properly fastened to the spars. On the mast, fine wire rings or loops of thread may be used. The jib should extend 9" up the stay (the "rope" from the end of the bowsprit to the top of the mast) and be either sewed to it or made to slide on it with small rings of wire.

Ballast can be cut (with tin-shears or saw) from lead pipe and nailed to the keel. To drive brads thru lead, pinch them between the thumb and finger, and drive them gently.

For convenience in holding the boat when it is out of the water, make a dry dock as shown in the drawing.

BOAT

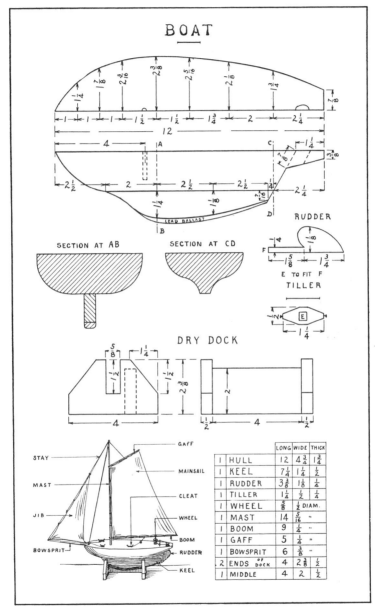

SECTION AT AB

SECTION AT CD

RUDDER

E TO FIT F

TILLER

DRY DOCK

LEAD BALLAST

		LONG	WIDE	THICK
1	HULL	12	$4\frac{3}{4}$	$1\frac{3}{4}$
1	KEEL	$7\frac{1}{4}$	$1\frac{1}{4}$	$\frac{1}{2}$
1	RUDDER	$3\frac{3}{8}$	$1\frac{1}{8}$	$\frac{1}{4}$
1	TILLER	$1\frac{1}{4}$	$\frac{1}{2}$	$\frac{1}{4}$
1	WHEEL	$\frac{5}{8}$	$\frac{1}{2}$ DIAM.	
1	MAST	14	$\frac{5}{16}$	"
1	BOOM	9	$\frac{1}{4}$	"
1	GAFF	5	$\frac{1}{4}$	"
1	BOWSPRIT	6	$\frac{3}{8}$	"
2	ENDS OF DOCK	4	$2\frac{3}{8}$	$\frac{1}{2}$
1	MIDDLE	4	2	$\frac{1}{2}$

STAY — MAST — JIB — BOWSPRIT — KEEL — RUDDER — BOOM — WHEEL — CLEAT — MAINSAIL — GAFF

PLATE 30

PILE-DRIVER—PLATE 31.

In wet, soft soil, wherever any building operations are to be undertaken, long, straight logs called piles have first to be driven to support the foundation. In wet soil they never rot; those driven for the building of Venice centuries ago are still solid. If holes are bored in the weight of this toy pile-driver, it is made more effective.

This is not a difficult model if each part is well made. It is important, however, to nail it in the following order: Runs to uprights, uprights to sides, sides to base, top to uprights, braces to uprights, then to base. The ends of the braces are mitered, that is, sawed, like the corner of a picture-frame, on the diagonal of a square. The axle of the little spool is made by two 1″ brads, and it rests in notches as near the end of the top blocks as is convenient to file them. It is held in place by little brads, or pins crossed over it, or by a staple made of a pin. A crank for the big spool (called the drum) is made of a 3″ piece of stiff wire. It should be flattened enough not to turn in the drum. Fasten the string to the drum thru a little hole drilled thru its rim. If the string comes off the upper spool, put a large screw-eye into the top piece and pass the string thru it.

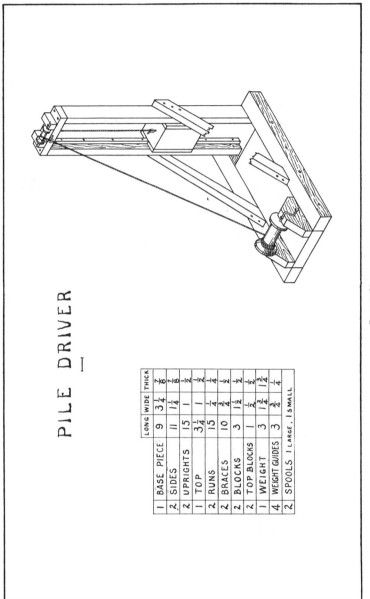

PILE DRIVER

		LONG	WIDE	THICK
1	BASE PIECE	9	$3\frac{1}{4}$	$\frac{7}{8}$
2	SIDES	11	$1\frac{1}{4}$	$\frac{7}{8}$
2	UPRIGHTS	15	1	$\frac{1}{2}$
1	TOP	$3\frac{1}{4}$	1	$\frac{1}{2}$
2	RUNS	15	$\frac{1}{4}$	$\frac{1}{4}$
2	BRACES	10	$\frac{3}{4}$	$\frac{1}{2}$
2	BLOCKS	3	$1\frac{1}{2}$	$\frac{1}{2}$
2	TOP BLOCKS	1	$\frac{1}{2}$	$\frac{1}{2}$
1	WEIGHT	3	$1\frac{3}{4}$	$1\frac{3}{4}$
4	WEIGHT GUIDES	3	$\frac{3}{4}$	$\frac{1}{4}$
2	SPOOLS	1 LARGE, 1 SMALL		

PLATE 31

WINDMILL—PLATE 32.

On a hilltop, exposed to every wind that blows, one of these windmills made by a boy has been spinning around for four years. The windmill in this form serves also as a weathervane. Pine is the best wood for this model. To withstand the weather, the model should be painted.

After planing the post to size, lay out the chamfers (see page 32) with a pencil on all four sides. The curve should be cut with a knife; the upper part may be planed, if the square part is not squeezed in the vise. Plane the two pieces for the vanes as accurately as possible so as to be able to make a good joint. Lay out and cut this joint as directed on page 24. After it is well fitted, draw the curves where the edges are to be whittled away. There are sixteen of them. Open the compass $\frac{3}{4}''$ and place the needle point always on the *front right-hand* edge as the wheel turns around. The curve begins $\frac{1}{8}''$ from the joint and ends $\frac{1}{8}''$ from the back edge (one also goes towards the lower edge). From this point draw a straight line to the end of the vane. Draw such lines as explained on page 32. Take the joint apart and whittle the edges away to these curves.

On the beam, make chamfers $1\frac{3}{4}''$ long. At the rear end, on the top and bottom, draw a center-line and two lines on each side of the center-line $\frac{1}{8}''$ apart. Between the first two, nearest the center-line, make the V-shaped groove in which the rudder fits. The sides of the beam are to be pared away to the other two lines, leaving this end $\frac{1}{2}''$ wide.

The curves at the rear end of the rudder can be sawed best with a scroll saw. Lacking that, proceed as follows: First, bore a $\frac{1}{4}''$ hole near the short straight line in the middle. Resting the rudder on a cutting board, pare to this line with a chisel. Next, saw straight from the end of the rudder to this straight line; then saw the corners, and pare to the curves. The width of the notch at the front end of the rudder is equal to the space left between the roots of the V-shaped notches in the beam. Measure this space, lay out the

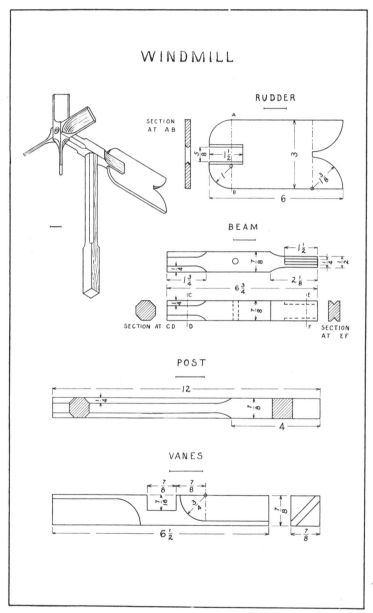

WINDMILL

RUDDER

SECTION AT AB

BEAM

SECTION AT CD

SECTION AT EF

POST

VANES

PLATE 32

notch, saw, and chisel it; then pare the corners so as to fit the V-shaped notches in the beam. Beware of crowding the rudder, for it will split easily. When fitted, glue and nail it in place, slanting a 1″ brad thru the curve into the beam.

Put the wheel on the beam with two washers and a large screw (2″ No. 12 round head is a good one). For this screw bore a ¼″ hole thru the center of the wheel, and a smaller hole in the beam. Now balance the windmill on the top of the post, and put the beam and post together with washers and screw in the same manner.

KITE-STRING REEL—PLATE 33.

A boy who flies kites will appreciate this reel for hauling in his kite quickly and keeping the string in order. The axle is made long for the purpose of putting on a brake when letting out a kite. The brake is simply a strong cord, fastened to a screw in the lower part of the further upright, (as viewed in Plate 33) wound several times around the axle, and the other end held in the hand. A 1" hole is bored in the base so that the reel can be anchored to the ground with a stake. With a loop of string fastened to the upright below the crank, the crank can be kept from turning, if one does not wish to let out all of the kite-string.

Make the base first, then the uprights. In the uprights, it is more convenient to bore the 9/16" holes before the sides are planed slanting. After the wheel pieces are joined in the manner explained on page 24, lay out the slanting lines on each arm while the joint is still together; then take it apart and plane to the slanting lines. Hold each piece securely slantwise in the vise, because one pair especially is apt to split from the notch outward. When this planing is finished, glue the joint and bore a $\frac{1}{2}$" hole straight thru the center. If convenient, make the cross pieces in one long piece, 20", planing off one corner flat (see sectional drawing, Plate 33) within $\frac{1}{8}$" of the two adjacent corners. Being careful to drive no brad into the $\frac{1}{2}$" hole, glue and nail these four cross pieces to one wheel. Then glue them to the other wheel and wind some string around tightly enough to hold this wheel while adjusting and nailing it. It will require care to get the cross pieces square with the first wheel, and the second wheel parallel with the first. After the string is wound around to hold the second wheel, measure the distance from wheel to wheel at the ends of all the arms. The nailing can be done while one arm of the wheels is held in the vise. The axle and handle should be glued and nailed to the crank. Now put the reel together, not forgetting the washers inside the uprights, and lock the wheels to the axle by drilling a hole for a 2" nail thru cross piece, wheel, and axle. (See illustration on page 55.)

– 8

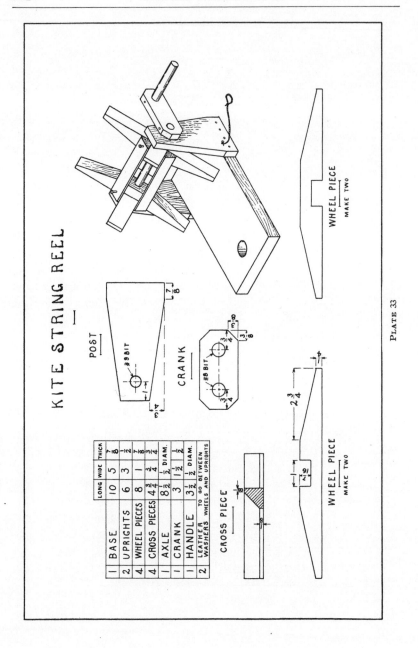

KITE STRING REEL

POST

CRANK

CROSS PIECE

WHEEL PIECE
MAKE TWO

WHEEL PIECE
MAKE TWO

	LONG	WIDE	THICK
1 BASE	10	5	$\frac{7}{8}$
2 UPRIGHTS	6	3	$\frac{1}{2}$
4 WHEEL PIECES	8	1	$\frac{7}{8}$
4 CROSS PIECES	$4\frac{3}{4}$	$\frac{3}{4}$	$\frac{3}{4}$
1 AXLE	$8\frac{1}{2}$	$\frac{1}{2}$ DIAM.	
1 CRANK	3	$1\frac{1}{2}$	$\frac{1}{2}$
1 HANDLE	$3\frac{1}{2}$	$\frac{1}{2}$ DIAM.	
2 LEATHER	TO GO BETWEEN		
WASHERS	WHEELS AND UPRIGHTS		

PLATE 33

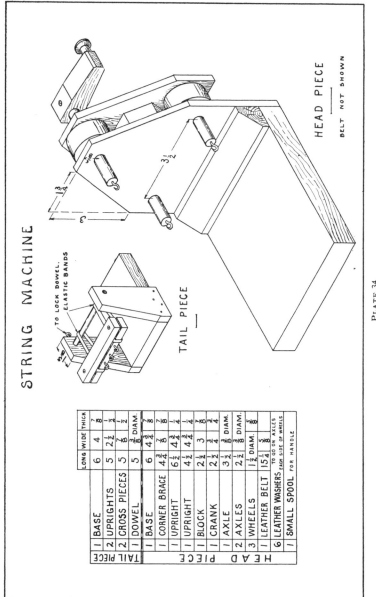

STRING MACHINE

HEAD PIECE

BELT NOT SHOWN

TAIL PIECE

PLATE 34

		LONG	WIDE	THICK
TAIL PIECE	1 BASE	6	4	$\frac{7}{8}$
	2 UPRIGHTS	5	$2\frac{1}{2}$	$\frac{1}{2}$
	2 CROSS PIECES	5	$\frac{7}{8}$	$\frac{1}{2}$
	1 DOWEL	5	$\frac{3}{8}$ DIAM.	
HEAD PIECE	1 BASE	6	$4\frac{3}{4}$	$\frac{7}{8}$
	1 CORNER BRACE	$4\frac{3}{4}$	$\frac{7}{8}$	$\frac{7}{8}$
	1 UPRIGHT	$6\frac{1}{2}$	$4\frac{3}{4}$	$\frac{1}{4}$
	1 UPRIGHT	$4\frac{1}{2}$	$4\frac{3}{4}$	$\frac{1}{4}$
	1 BLOCK	$2\frac{1}{2}$	3	$\frac{7}{8}$
	1 CRANK	$2\frac{1}{2}$	$\frac{3}{4}$	$\frac{3}{4}$
	1 AXLE	$3\frac{1}{2}$	$\frac{3}{8}$ DIAM.	
	2 AXLES	$2\frac{1}{2}$	$\frac{3}{8}$ DIAM.	
	3 WHEELS	$1\frac{1}{2}$ DIAM.		$\frac{5}{8}$
	1 LEATHER BELT	$15\frac{1}{4}$	$\frac{5}{8}$	
	6 LEATHER WASHERS	TO GO ON AXLES EACH SIDE OF WHEELS		
	1 SMALL SPOOL	FOR HANDLE		

STRING MACHINE—Plate 34.

On a machine like this, one can twist bowstrings, topstrings, fishlines, silk cord for fancy work, and any similar cord. Tho designed to be held on the floor or table with flat-irons, clamps, of course, will hold it better.

Make the tail piece first. In the cross pieces of the tail piece are two screws ⅞″ from the ends; be careful to bore the holes large enough so the screws will not split them. The edges of the lower cross piece must be sandpapered enough not to cut the elastic bands.

In order that the belt shall run on the center of the wheels in the head piece, it is important to have the three axles parallel. To make them so, the two uprights must be clamped together while boring the ⅜″ holes for the axles. Lest the spur of the bit split the uprights, drill small holes at each center first. Do not nail the longer upright to the base until the belt runs well in both directions. On a lathe, the wheels and axles could easily be made of one piece; lacking a lathe, a big spool or curtain pole must be used. Plug the hole of the spool with a dowel, then very accurately find its center and bore a ⅜″ hole thru it. Saw it into three ⅝″ pieces for the wheels. Glue these to the axles so that 1″ extends thru the taller upright. A belt runs better on a wheel that is "crowned," that is, slightly larger in the middle; so the edges of these wheels must be pared 1/32″, making a gentle curve. Put the washers each side of the wheels, then put the wheels in place in the taller upright, and nail this to the triangular block. Pull a ⅝″ leather belt tightly around the three wheels and sew the ends so that they butt together. Clamp the shorter upright in position and turn the upper axle to see if the belt runs well in both directions. It will run true when all three axles are parallel, so keep knocking the shorter upright from side to side or up and down until the belt does run true; then bore holes for three screws to hold it to the triangular block. Make the crank and lock it to the upper axle with a ½″ screw.

To twist a string, set the two parts of the machine somewhat farther apart than the finished length desired, put on as many threads, from hooks on the tail piece to corresponding hooks on the head piece, as will make the finished string the desired size. Observe how these separate threads were twisted, and start the machine in the *opposite* way. Twist until the three strands kink readily when the head piece is brought nearer the tail piece. The tighter these are twisted, the harder the string will be. (Soap rubbed on the inside of the belt may make the belt carry more power). When these three strands are twisted enough, remove the two lower ones from their *hooks on the head piece* to the upper hook. Twist in the *opposite* direction until the string kinks again, and it is made. If the three strands are waxed, a stronger string will be made.

WINDMILL FORCE-PUMP—Plate 35.

If this pump is properly connected with an air chamber, as explained later, it will send a small stream of water some ten feet. In a gale, the windmill is strong enough, in fact, to force the valves from the glass tubes. Like any model of considerable mechanism, this will require patience to get it in working order. The post is made short for stability. If it can be held in place firmly, a trestle-work tower like a real windmill might be built of stock $\frac{1}{2}''$x$\frac{1}{2}''$ for the corner posts and $\frac{1}{2}''$x$\frac{1}{8}''$ for the braces.

The post is slanting on two sides to fit the journals at the top. It is fastened to the base with two $2''$ screws. Make the wheel center $2\frac{1}{8}''$ square, and thru its center bore a $\frac{1}{4}''$ hole. If it does not revolve true, make another block and try again. Make the block octagonal by cutting off each corner $\frac{5}{8}''$. On each of the eight faces saw notches $\frac{1}{8}''$ wide and $5/16''$ deep into which the vanes will fit. (See page 64 on cutting notches.) Make and glue the vanes in place and lay the wheel flat to dry.

Procure three pieces of water-gage glass $2''$ long, $7/16''$ to $\frac{1}{2}''$ inside diameter. Glass tubes can be broken apart by filing a slight notch, grasping the tube firmly each side of the notch, and pulling and bending the tube away from the notch. If the file starts a little break, this will be comparatively easy, if it does not, file some more. Into two tubes little valves must be cemented. These can be made of a firm piece of leather. Sole leather that is not too hard is best. With knife or chisel, pare two pieces on the cutting board to fit in the tubes. The cement will make them water tight later. Push the sharp point of a penknife into the smooth side of the leather disk and make a circular cut, as one would remove a speck from an apple, but do not cut the flap completely out, because it must be left hinged to the disk. Turn this flap up straight out of the way so as to be able to work a $\frac{1}{4}''$ hole thru the disk. This can be punched, drilled, or cut out with a $\frac{1}{8}''$ chisel, and finished with a penknife. Of course, the edges of the flap should cover this hole completely. The valve in the lowest tube should be cemented about $\frac{1}{2}''$ from the lower

WINDMILL FORCE-PUMP

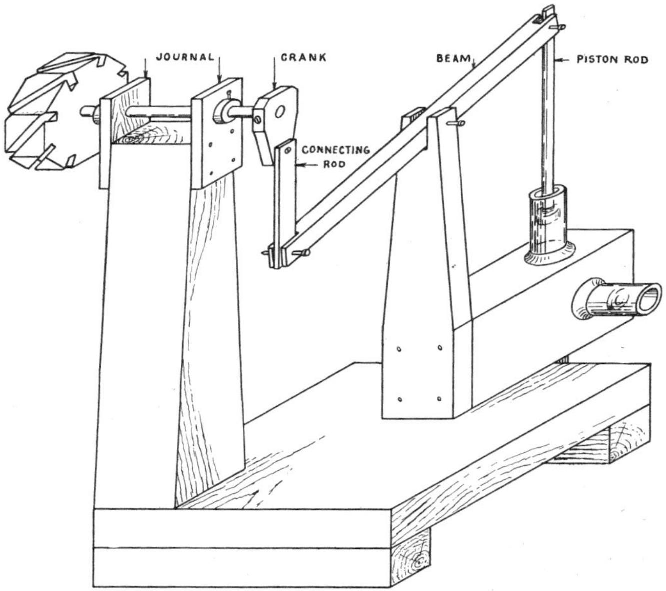

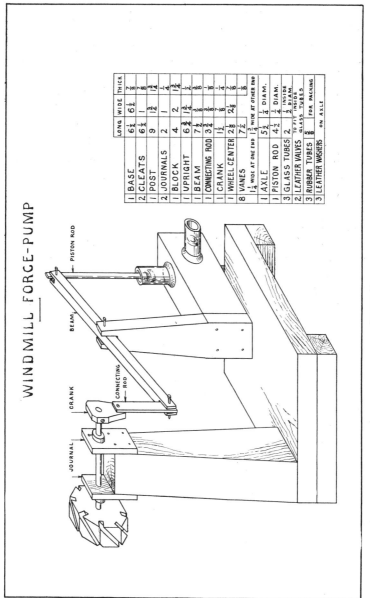

		LONG	WIDE	THICK
1	BASE	$6\frac{1}{2}$	$6\frac{1}{2}$	$\frac{7}{8}$
2	CLEATS	$6\frac{1}{2}$	1	$\frac{7}{8}$
1	POST	9	$1\frac{3}{4}$	$1\frac{3}{4}$
2	JOURNALS	2	1	$\frac{1}{4}$
1	BLOCK	4	2	$1\frac{3}{4}$
1	UPRIGHT	$6\frac{3}{4}$	$1\frac{3}{4}$	$\frac{1}{2}$
1	BEAM	$7\frac{1}{2}$	$\frac{3}{8}$	$\frac{3}{8}$
1	CONNECTING ROD	$3\frac{3}{4}$	$\frac{3}{8}$	$\frac{1}{8}$
1	CRANK	$1\frac{1}{2}$	$\frac{7}{8}$	$\frac{1}{4}$
1	WHEEL CENTER	$2\frac{1}{8}$	$2\frac{1}{8}$	$\frac{7}{8}$
8	VANES	$7\frac{1}{2}$		$\frac{1}{8}$
	$1\frac{1}{4}$ WIDE AT ONE END	$1\frac{3}{4}$ WIDE AT OTHER END		
1	AXLE	$5\frac{1}{2}$	$\frac{1}{4}$ DIAM.	
1	PISTON ROD	$4\frac{1}{2}$	$\frac{1}{4}$ DIAM.	
3	GLASS TUBES	2	$\frac{1}{2}$ INSIDE DIAM.	
2	LEATHER VALVES	TO FIT INSIDE GLASS TUBES		
3	RUBBER TUBES	$\frac{5}{8}$	FOR PACKING	
3	LEATHER WASHERS	ON AXLE		

PLATE 35

end with the flap up, that in the horizontal tube about ¾″ from the outer end with the flap out. To make sealing-wax sticky enough to cement these valves in the tubes, melt one teaspoon of wax with one-half teaspoon of turpentine in a large spoon, and allow it to cool. Break it in pieces small enough to go in the tubes. Put the valve in the tube a little to one side of its final position; put in some of the wax mixture; heat the tube in an alcohol flame, rolling the tube till the wax begins to melt; remove from the flame; and when the wax is all melted, push the valve to its final position with a pencil. While it is cooling, see that the wax does not flow into the valve. All three tubes must have a piece of rubber tubing on the outside to serve as packing in the wooden block. With an expansive bit, holes can be bored in the block so that the rubber tubing will fit tightly. Lacking that, bore a smaller hole and enlarge it with a round file. The center of the vertical hole is somewhat to the left (as viewed in Plate 35) of the center of the block to allow the horizontal tube more support. This will require the notch in the upright also to be to the left of the center. After the holes are bored, the pores of the wood must be filled with paraffin. In a little dish, melt some paraffin and put it into the holes with a rag tied to a stick. When the holes are well covered, drive the wax into the wood with an alcohol or candle flame held in the hole till the wood is fairly hot. The outside of the block might well be treated in like manner. It will be best to cement these tubes in their places. Melt a tablespoon of sealing wax with about as much turpentine. With this, not too hot, build up a good fillet over the rubber tubing ¼″, perhaps, on the glass tubes.

Make a good fitting piston for the upper tube; it must not slide hard (oil it) and yet it must be air tight. To make the piston file two grooves ½″ apart around and near the end of the piston rod. Wind a hummock of yarn between these grooves till it almost fills the tube, then wrap a piece of soft cloth (knitted underwear) smoothly over the hummock, tying it in each groove with thread.

Lock the crank to the axle with a $\frac{1}{2}''$ screw. Adjust the axle and keep it in position with two leather washers locked to the axle just outside the journals. Clamp the block to the base, adjust it in line with the crank, and fasten it with two $1\frac{1}{2}''$ screws up thru the base. The last connection to make is between the crank and connecting-rod. To make this, raise the piston to its highest position, and turn the crank to its lowest; choose what seems the best point for the screw, marking the point on crank and connecting-rod; now lower the piston and raise the crank; if the two points do not come together, the screw should be placed half way between them. This screw should be tight in the crank. The wheel can now be glued to the axle or locked with a brad slanting from the front of the wheel center.

Before they will work, the valves must be made limber with water, and to start the pump, water may have to be put on each side of the valves. Water may be pumped to any height by fastening a pipe to the horizontal tube. To obtain a steady stream, like a fire-engine, connect the horizontal tube with an air-tight bottle. The pipe which goes into this bottle should reach just below the stopper. The outlet pipe should nearly reach the bottom of the bottle, and it should have a nozzle smaller than any other opening in the whole apparatus. The bottle should be partly full of water. Quarter-inch glass tubing can be melted and shaped in an alcohol flame, and, if some rubber tubing is used as a connection, the nozzle can be played anywhere.